L. B. J.

The Man from Johnson City

L.B.J.

The Man from Johnson City

CLARKE NEWLON

Illustrated with photographs

REVISED AND ENLARGED EDITION

DODD, MEAD & COMPANY

NEW YORK

1970 Printing

ISBN 0-396-04983-4
Library of Congress Catalog Card Number: 72-135209

12, 369

Printed in the United States of America
by The Cornwall Press, Inc., Cornwall, N. Y.

Acknowledgments

It would be impossible to write a detailed, factual biography of a living President of the United States without his express approval to some degree. The writer must have access to too many records and personal papers which can only be had through the White House. He must draw on the recollections of too many friends, going back nearly half a century in some instances, for the events, small or great, which shaped the decisions and actions of the subject. The power of the Presidency is too great for friends, associates and members of the White House staff to risk, without this approval, the possibility of remembering something better forgotten.

With this in mind, the author acknowledges with thanks the acquiescence of President Lyndon B. Johnson that this book be written, and at the same time hastens to add that the manuscript was not read (except in small part) or cleared by the White House before publication, and that this is in no way an "authorized" biography.

The author is grateful to many of Mr. Johnson's old friends who took the time to recall details of their association: Russell Morton Brown, one of the earliest of the President's Washington friends; Jesse Kellam, Willard Deason, Charles Green and Sherman Birdwell of Austin; Judge A. W. Moursund and Mrs. J. B. ("Kittie") Leonard of Johnson City.

The author is also indebted to General Samuel Anderson, whose remarkable memory detailed the President's war exploits; to Thomas G. ("Tommy the Cork") Corcoran, for sharing his personal knowledge of the President's friendship with Franklin Roosevelt; to Kenneth BeLieu, Assistant Secretary of the Navy; to Dan Quill, the Postmaster of San Antonio, who bought Lady Bird's wedding ring; and to Booth Mooney, James Reston, Doris Fleeson, Sid Davis and Ilario Fiore (of Milan) who permitted quotations from their own writing. Finally, great appreciation is expressed to the hard-working White House staff members who took the time to both clear paths and help personally—George Reedy, Dorothy Jackson Nichols, Dorothy Territo, Dr. Edward Welsh, Arthur Perry, Walter Jenkins, Elizabeth Carpenter, Simone Poulain, Pierre Salinger, Malcolm Kilduff and Willie Day Taylor.

Thanks to Gwen Cammack for her invaluable chores of research on the early versions of this book, and to Ellen Hanna Simmons who assembled the material for the revised edition and helped greatly with the rewriting and reediting.

Clarke Newlon

Contents

Contents

Illustrations

ix

1

☆

Assassination: a New President

Vice President Lyndon Johnson rode in the third car of the motorcade as it approached the triple underpass which led to downtown Dallas. With him were his wife, Lady Bird, and Senator Ralph Yarborough of Texas. It was the sunny, hot Friday of November 22, 1963.

The three chatted casually and the Vice President waved at the crowds which had lined the road all the way from the airport. They were cheering, festive. It was a wonderful Texas welcome. Lyndon Johnson smiled as he saw a father lift a child to his shoulders for a better view of the President and Vice President of the United States.

Preceding the Johnson auto were two others. Directly in front was an open touring car filled with armed Secret Service men. Leading the parade into Dallas was the car which held President John F. Kennedy and Texas Governor John Connally, with their wives.

The shots, when they came in one rapid, measured burst, sounded like firecrackers. The President fell forward, struck twice. The other bullet hit the Governor. A woman, only a few feet away in the crowd, screamed, "My God! He's shot!" A newsman, looking up, saw what he thought to be the barrel of a rifle being withdrawn through the window of a building some seventy-five yards distant.

Rufus Youngblood, the Secret Service agent assigned to Johnson, threw the Vice President to the floor of the car and shielded him with his own body. In response to imperative shouts from the guards ahead, Mrs. Johnson and Senator Yarborough crouched in their seats. Then the car sped away, following the fatally wounded President to Dallas' Parkland Hospital.

Malcolm Kilduff, Assistant White House Press Secretary, was riding with newsmen in the car just behind the Vice President. He heard the shots and saw people in the crowd turn to run.

There was a flash of pink movement from the lead car. Mrs. Kennedy was wearing pink, Kilduff knew. He saw a Secret Service man raise his rifle. The story of what followed he told first over a Westinghouse network radio broadcast.

"I remember," said Kilduff, "seeing one cameraman off to the right running up the grassy slope to get pictures. I remember seeing one man push his child down. Then we went around the Johnson car because it had slowed down and we wanted to catch up with the President's car.

"At the entrance of Parkland Hospital we all jumped out and ran over to the Kennedy car. We saw President Kennedy lying on the seat. We saw Governor Connally spread on his back. Actually, Governor Connally looked at first glance to be in even worse shape than President Kennedy, because the bullet came out through his chest and he was just covered with blood on the front.

"But then, when you saw President Kennedy's head, you knew this was a fatal wound. But, you know, you couldn't think of this. I mean, it just doesn't occur to you that this man is going to be killed. It is an inconceivable thought."

Kilduff ran into the hospital to locate telephones for representatives of the press wire services.

"When I got back outside," he continued, "they had just taken Governor Connally out of the car. They had to get him out first to get President Kennedy out.

"Then they took President Kennedy out. His condition was pretty apparent. He was loaded on the stretcher and—one thing I haven't seen written—was the sight of Jacqueline Kennedy helping to push the stretcher through the halls, with her hair flying and [her clothes] dripping blood. To me, it was the most pathetic sight in the world."

A few minutes past one o'clock, Kilduff learned from Kenneth O'Donnell, a Presidential assistant, that President Kennedy was dead.

"Mrs. Kennedy was sitting directly outside of the Emergeny Room, just to the right," he recalls, "and just sitting there with her hands in her lap, with the most helpless look that any human could have on her face."

When a few moments more had passed, Kilduff went to O'Donnell and told him that the world would have to be told of the President's death. O'Donnell told him he should go ahead, but to check with Lyndon Johnson first.

Kilduff walked through the Emergency Room into the small cubicle where Mr. Johnson was sitting with Mrs. Johnson and Rufus Youngblood, the Secret Service man. O'Donnell had already broken the news to them.

"I walked up to him and, very frankly, I didn't know what to call him. I just blurted out: 'Mr. President.' I will never forget the look on his face. I am fairly sure that this was the first time he had been called 'Mr. President.'"

Kilduff told Lyndon Johnson that he would have to announce the death of President Kennedy, and asked: "Is it all right with you?"

The President replied: "No, Mac, I think we had better wait for a few minutes. I think I had better get out of here and back on the plane before you announce it."

Lyndon Johnson continued voicing the thoughts which must have been going through his mind on that day and hour of confusion and terrible tragedy.

"We don't know whether this is a world-wide conspiracy, whether they are after me as well as they were after President Kennedy; whether they were after Speaker McCormack, or Senator Hayden. We just don't know."

He revealed later that his thoughts had gone back in history to the assassination of President Lincoln and the attempt at that time on the life of Secretary of State Seward as well. Under present laws, the Speaker of the House (John McCormack) and the President pro tempore of the Senate (Carl Hayden), were next in the line of succession after the Vice President.

Kilduff went outside and found Roy Kellerman, the Secret Service agent in charge of the Texas trip. Kellerman rounded up an escort to take President Johnson to the airport. Then Kilduff walked out of the Emergency Entrance with the President, who got into his car and was driven off to the airport.

"It was," said Kilduff, "a scene of absolute confusion. Everyone was screaming at us, 'What can you tell us, what can you tell us?'"

When the President had gone, Kilduff ran up the sloping

lawn and into the hospital. There he met the press in a nurses' classroom. Half ill, half faint from emotion, he read from a slip of paper:

"President John F. Kennedy died at approximately 1:00 P.M., central standard time, from a gunshot in the brain here in Dallas."

Kilduff left the hospital immediately and was driven to the airport and the Presidential plane. The shades were drawn on all of the windows. As he walked into the rear compartment, President Johnson said to him:

"Mac, I have to get sworn in here. I have talked to Bobby [Attorney General Robert Kennedy] in Washington. He feels I should be sworn in here in Dallas. We are trying to get hold of a judge. Do we have to allow some of the press in here?" Kilduff told him he did.

Sid Davis, White House correspondent for the Westinghouse Broadcasting Company, was one of the newsmen who witnessed the swearing-in ceremony.

He had been at the hospital, filing his story on the official death announcement, and had stepped away from the phone for a second to ask a question. Edward ("Jiggs") Fauver, of the White House Transportation office, grabbed him by the arm.

"Come on with me," he said. "We need a pool [of newsmen]. Don't ask any questions."

"I grabbed my typewriter and left," related Davis. "We were joined by Merriman Smith of United Press International and Chuck Roberts of *Newsweek*.

"A police car rushed us to the airport without using its siren, so it wouldn't attract attention. The policeman radioed ahead to Air Force One (the Presidential Plane) to wait, that the reporters were on their way."

Davis remembers a brief pause at the plane entrance and a showing of credentials.

"It was very hot and stuffy on the airplane," he continued. "It had been sitting there all day and the temperature in Dallas, even when we had arrived, was seventy-five degrees.

"We were taken to the rear of the plane, into the reception room of the Presidential suite. This is a room, I would say, about fifteen by twelve." There were about thirty people in the room. President Johnson was there with Mrs. Johnson. Many of the others were Kennedy staff people, including old Kennedy friends—Larry O'Brien, Dave Powers and Kenny O'Donnell. There were also Johnson staffers Bill Moyers and Jack Valenti.

"We seemed to be waiting for someone," said Davis, "and in a few seconds, Mrs. Kennedy came into the room from the rear compartment, where she had been sitting with the casket of her husband, and where she had been trying to compose herself so that she could attend the ceremony."

The scene remains vividly clear to Davis. He remembers: "I think everybody in the room just stopped. No one even breathed at that moment. They just looked at her. The thing which stands out in my mind, I think, out of the entire ceremony, was when I looked at Mrs. Kennedy, and she had come into the room, she was still wearing that raspberry two-piece suit, that beautiful suit that looks so well on her, and the lower part of the skirt was still soaked with the blood of the President, and her left stocking was just saturated with blood.

"Her large eyes just looked at everybody. She was bewildered, shocked, and just seemed to be confused, and her face seemed to say to all of us, 'Why?' "

The new President placed the widow of the late President on his left and told Federal Judge Sarah Hughes, an old friend, to proceed with the ceremony. He asked for ice water. It was brought and he took two sips. Judge Hughes told the President to raise his right hand and he repeated after her:

"I do solemnly swear that I will faithfully execute the office of the President of the United States, and will to the best of my ability preserve, protect and defend the Constitution of the United States."

At the moment of the oath-taking, Davis set the second hand on his watch. He timed it at twenty-eight seconds.

The ceremony ended, the President gently embraced Mrs. Kennedy and his wife. And then he said:

"O.K., let's get this plane back to Washington." The departure time was 2:47 P.M.

Mrs. Kennedy retired to the rear compartment for her lonely vigil over the casket of her murdered husband. Later, she asked that O'Brien, Powers and O'Donnell join her and they did.

The newsmen, of course, and many of the other witnesses to the ceremony left the plane. Malcolm Kilduff remained aboard and accompanied the President to Washington.

"President Johnson reacted to the situation in terms of a national emergency," he said. "All the way back he was planning on whom he should meet with immediately; whom he should call together immediately; to get Rusk back immediately." (Secretary of State Dean Rusk and several other cabinet members, en route to Japan, checked their flight in mid-air and returned.) Johnson also arranged for an immediate Cabinet meeting, a conference with Congressional leaders and an intelligence briefing.

"He called Mrs. Rose Kennedy [the late President's mother] from the aircraft. He called Governor Connally's wife from the aircraft. He wanted an immediate intelligence report from McGeorge Bundy and Robert McNamara [White House assistant and Secretary of Defense] as soon as we hit ground."

When the Presidential plane reached Andrews Air Force Base that evening, Jackie Kennedy followed the casket into the waiting ambulance and rode with it into the city. Robert Kennedy met the plane and rode with her.

President Johnson alighted then, and was greeted by leading Congressmen from both parties, McNamara, Under Secretary of State George Ball and White House Aide McGeorge Bundy. He spoke briefly into the microphones:

"This is a sad time for all the people. We have suffered a loss that cannot be weighed. For me it is a deep personal tragedy. I know the world shares the sorrow that Mrs. Kennedy and her family bear. I will do my best. That is all I can do. I ask for your help and God's."

McNamara, Bundy and Ball accompanied Lyndon Johnson back to the White House in a helicopter.

His first official act as President was to declare Monday, November 25, the day of John F. Kennedy's burial, a day of national mourning throughout the United States.

The President's first tactical move after taking office was to retain the team John Kennedy had built up over his three years. That he was able to do it in large part is a tribute both to the sincerity and power of his appeal, and to the deep integrity of the Kennedy staff.

The President's appeal to all of them was virtually the

same one sentence: "I need you worse than he did." He voiced it first to McNamara, Bundy and Ball during the helicopter flight from Andrews Air Force Base, on the evening of November 22. He repeated it in the days that followed.

The "Irish Mafia" of Massachusetts-bred brains which John F. Kennedy had gathered around him were singularly personal in their loyalty. They might easily have left. So might Attorney General Robert Kennedy. He, perhaps, more than the others, realized how much they were needed. Had he left, the others might have followed, but when he stuck to the job, so did they. Of all the men on the old Kennedy team, President Johnson is probably most grateful to the slain President's brother, even though the two men had great personal and political differences otherwise.

The President had many and good reasons for wanting to keep these men. For one thing, he couldn't have built up an equally competent staff in months. There was the need to counter the effect abroad of the assassination of an American President. If the Kennedy team deserted the White House, any picture of orderly transition in the government would have been destroyed in foreign eyes. Also, the appearance of uninterrupted continuity in the Kennedy program would have been seriously damaged on the home front.

As a result of the new President's success with White House staffers, Cabinet members and other key job holders, plus his own deeply professional competence in politics, the transition was far smoother than any previously recorded in history. The Johnson moves were sure-footed.

His first week in office was one of sandwich lunches and little sleep. He conferred with the Cabinet. Congressional leaders found themselves invited to breakfast. He prefaced a cut in government expenses by sharply limiting the limousine allowance of federal agencies and the military. He announced he would address the United Nations. He delivered a message to a joint assembly of Congress on November 27 which was half a eulogy to the late President Kennedy and half a rededication of Kennedy-Johnson policy. In urging passage of civil rights and tax reduction measures, he used the word "action" so many times it created comment in the press. He told the combined Senate and House:

"All I have I would have given gladly not to be standing here today.

"The greatest leader of our time has been struck down by the foulest deed of our time. Today, John Fitzgerald Kennedy lives on in the immortal words and works that he left behind.

"The dream of conquering the vastness of space—the dream of partnership across the Atlantic—and across the Pacific as well—the dream of a Peace Corps in less developed nations—the dream of education for all of our children—the dream of jobs for all who seek them and need them—the dream of care for our elderly—the dream of an all-out attack on mental illness—and above all, the dream of equal rights for all Americans, whatever their race or color—these and other American dreams have been vitalized by his drive and by his dedication.

"And now the ideas and ideals which he so nobly represented must and will be translated into effective action.

"Our most immediate tasks are here on this Hill. First, no memorial oration or eulogy could more eloquently honor President Kennedy's memory than the earliest possible passage of the civil rights bill for which he fought so long. We have talked long enough in this country about equal rights. We have talked for one hundred years or more. It is time now to write the next chapter, and to write it in the books of law.

"I urge you again, as I did in 1957 and again in 1960, to enact a civil rights law so that we can move forward to eliminate from this Nation every trace of discrimination and oppression that is based upon race or color. There could be no greater source of strength to this Nation, both at home and abroad.

"And second, no act of ours could more fittingly continue the work of President Kennedy than the early passage of the tax bill for which he fought all this long year. This is a bill designed to increase our national income and Federal revenues, and to provide insurance against recession. That bill, if passed without delay, means more security for those now working, more jobs for those now without them, and more incentive for our economy.

"In short, this is no time for delay. It is a time for action —strong, forward-looking action on the pending education bills to help bring the light of learning to every home and hamlet in America—strong, forward-looking action on youth employment opportunities; strong, forward-looking action on the pending foreign aid bill, making clear that we are not forfeiting our responsibilities to this hemisphere or to the world, nor erasing executive flexibility in the conduct of our foreign affairs—and strong, prompt and forward-looking action on the remaining appropriations bills.

Lyndon Johnson's support of the civil rights measure was so forceful it moved Whitney Young, Jr., Executive Director of the National Urban League, to comment:

"Ten years ago, if we had heard a new President speaking in a deep Southern drawl, there might have been so much fear among Negro leaders that some of us might have gotten on the next boat for Ghana.

"But we know where Lyndon Johnson stands and we realize that he is a sincere and dedicated supporter of civil rights. A magnolia accent doesn't always mean bigotry."

On the foreign affairs front, the President arranged for visits to the United States of Germany's Chancellor Erhard, Britain's Sir Alec Douglas-Home, Italy's President Segni, Canada's Lester Pearson and Mexico's President Adolfo Lopez Mateos. Notably absent from any mention was France's President DeGaulle, who had indicated he would prefer that Johnson come to see him.

Lyndon Johnson told the United Nations that America would stay close to the course which had been charted there by John Kennedy three months earlier, and in hoping for an end to the Cold War, he repeated the late President's words: "Peace is a journey of one thousand miles and it must be taken one step at a time."

President Johnson announced a "War on Poverty" and named Sargent Shriver a special White House Assistant to organize and administer an agency for a major assault on this age-old problem, its causes and cures. Shriver, a Kennedy brother-in-law, had been notably successful in building the Peace Corps, the brightest star in the Administration crown. The Washington press immediately dubbed the new agency the "Poor Corps."

The President named an advisory board for this "unconditional war," composed of the Secretaries of Health, Education and Welfare, of Labor, the Interior, and Agriculture, in addition to the Attorney General. As Shriver put a borrowed staff of experts into round-the-clock sessions to forge a program, the President gave the assignment added weight by addressing this directive to him:

"Since this campaign against poverty will be an important part of the work of the Cabinet, I am asking you to attend all its meetings."

To Congress, he said:

"Poverty is a national problem, requiring improved national organization and support. But this attack, to be effective, must also be organized at the State and local level and must be supported and directed by State and local efforts, for the war against poverty will not be won in Washington. It must be won in the field, in every private home, in every public office, from the courthouse to the White House.

"The program I shall propose will emphasize this cooperative approach to help that one-fifth of all American families with incomes too small to even meet their basic needs.

"Our chief weapons in a more pinpointed attack will be better schools and better health, better homes, better training and better job opportunities to help more Americans, especially young Americans, escape from squalor and misery and unemployment rolls where other citizens help to carry them.

"Very often a lack of jobs and money is not the cause of poverty, but the symptom. The cause may lie deeper, in our failure to give our fellow citizens a fair chance to develop their own capacities, in a lack of education and training, in a lack of medical care and housing, in a lack of decent communities in which to live and bring up their children."

Chancellor Erhard arrived during the Christmas holidays of 1963 and was entertained at the LBJ ranch with music and a barbecue. At this "spare-ribs summit," thoughtful host Lyndon Johnson brought a choral group from nearby Fredericksburg to sing for the German guest of honor *"Tief in das Herz von* Texas," followed by Beethoven and Brahms from another Texan who had made good, pianist Van Cliburn.

In his State of the Union message, delivered on January 8, 1964, President Johnson asked Congress to carry forward the plans and programs of John Fitzgerald Kennedy, "not because of our sorrow or sympathy, but because they are right."

He asked for an expansion of area redevelopment and legislation which would put "jobless, aimless, hopeless youngsters to work on useful projects." He proposed extending the coverage of the minimum wage law and hospital insurance for older citizens through Social Security. He urged again the passage of the civil rights and the tax reduction bills.

He produced the greatest triumph of the transition period by coming up with a proposed 1965-66 budget of $97.9 billion—from two to three and a half billion dollars less than the experts had predicted.

As part of his State of the Union message, the President described this budget to Congress in the following words:

"I pledge a progressive Administration which is efficient, and honest and frugal. The budget to be submitted to the Congress shortly is in full accord with this pledge.

"It will cut our deficit in half—from $10 billion to $4 billion 900 million. It will be in proportion to our national output, the smallest budget since 1951.

"It will call for a substantial reduction in Federal employment, a feat accomplished only once before in the last ten years.

"While maintaining the full strength of our combat defenses, it will call for the lowest number of civilian personnel in the Department of Defense since 1950.

"It will call for total expenditures of $97 billion 900 million—compared to $98 billion 400 million for the current year, a reduction of more than $500 million."

Mindful as ever of national defense, he said that our margin of safety and superiority in both conventional and unconventional weapons would be maintained. We shall, he said, make new proposals toward the control and eventual abolition of arms, and noted that he had directed the closing of many nonessential American military installations.

He proposed the increased use of food as an instrument of peace, whether by sale, trade, loan or donation to hungry people of all nations. He gave assurances of our continued pre-eminence in the peaceful exploration of space and pledged expansion of our world trade.

George Reedy, the President's longtime man of all work, lists five early—and major—accomplishments of the Johnson Administration in its first few months. They are:

1. The smooth, effective transition of power from John Kennedy to Lyndon Johnson.

2. Getting the nation so absorbed in the action which was coming out of Washington it forgot its own trouble. People, shocked and grief-stricken over the assassination, "forgot to cry," said Reedy.

3. The war on poverty. "Lyndon Johnson understands poverty," said Reedy. "His own poverty was rural, but he

has seen enough of it elsewhere to understand that it is the same, rural or urban."

4. Cutting the ground out from under the Republican Party. With a reduced budget, how can you make an issue out of a tax cut?

5. Getting Congress moving. Considering its record of 1963, this was a notable achievement, particularly when the Senate and House moved to pass the civil rights bill virtually intact and a tax reduction measure which was at least acceptable to the Administration.

The early months, however, were not without their losses. Foreign aid, in which the President believes passionately, took its licks. When Congress cut the appropriation from the original four and half million to three, he spoke in sharp frustration:

"I don't seem to do any better with Congress than other people."

Foreign problems, too, seemed determined to rise plaguily. An unexpected coup in Vietnam, anti-Americanism in Saigon, a leftist takeover in Zanzibar, the Greek-Turkish conflicts on Cyprus and rioting in the Panama over the Canal treaty were none of them major crises in this nuclear age, when considered singly, but their accumulated impact has been serious. They have presented no easy solutions, either. Johnson has said: "It takes time to make progress."

When Lyndon Johnson had been in the White House two weeks, Columnist James Reston wrote in the *New York Times:*

"President Johnson's strength is that he can outwork, outtalk, and outwit almost any other member of the human race, and this is also his greatest weakness. For he gets results by application of a technique that is a menace to his health and therefore to the continuity of his government.

"Lyndon Johnson wins at politics for the same reason that Texas wins at football. He overwhelms the opponent with power. You know exactly where he's going but he rolls over you anyway. And the only difference between him and the number one football team in the country is that he would like to call all the signals, carry the ball on every play and run his own interference."

Actually, those close to the President do not try to cut down on his activities as much as they try to regulate them. Under the advice of his doctors, Rear Admiral George Burkley, White House physician, and Dr. Willis Hurst at Bethesda Naval Hospital, President Johnson maintains something close to an orderly life, strenuous though it may be.

He is normally out of bed by six-thirty or seven in the morning and will spend the next hour reading several newspapers, which he goes through rapidly but thoroughly, frequently querying aides later about items which may appear in unlikely places, the women's page, for instance. He also examines keenly the Congressional Record. The Record is, and has been for years, his source for determining the moods, trends and temper of Congress.

Breakfast will include his own ranch-cured bacon from the LBJ ranch, or venison sausage from there, eggs and home-baked bread. By this time it is around nine o'clock and the "system" takes over—appointments, meetings, official duties.

Lunch follows a mandatory—almost—daily swim in the White House pool, usually accompanied by one or more of the White House aides. The President likes to swim but is no champ; he dog paddles mostly. The White House pool is co-educational. Mrs. Johnson and the two daughters use it at times, and occasionally some of the "in-family" girl secretaries—when the President is away and they know the coast is clear.

The President is an *aficionado* of Mexican food and would probably eat chili, enchiladas, ranch style beans, barbecue and *jalapeños* twice a day if he didn't have a sensible diet, and other members of the family, to consider. (*Jalapeños* are Mexican peppers of varying degrees of heat.) He also likes hamburgers, floating island pudding, ice cream and the small but well-flavored peaches which come from the LBJ country. (The village of Stonewall, just across the Pedernales River from the ranch, brags that it is the peach center of Southwest Texas.)

Lunch is at one, and after it the system, or the President's sixteen-button telephone, again commands his life. There are a hundred details to master for a hundred decisions; conferences with aides, meetings, a speech to go over, a problem from State or Defense, a Senator to be wooed for an important vote; a crucial issue with labor or industry, a briefing, a report. If it can be squeezed into the schedule, Johnson naps for thirty minutes at four or four-thirty and then back to his desk. Official dinners occupy the President and First Lady as many as five nights a week, but official or otherwise, dinner is at a reasonable hour. He used to work through the dinner hour and then bolt a big meal just before going to bed. Because of his heart attack, his doctors have put a complete prohibition on this. (The heart wants to slow down with sleep, but a full stomach keeps it working away.)

Bedtime is about 11:30 and there is always a stack of memoranda on the bedside table which the President will read until two in the morning. During the office day he wants short, half-page briefing notes, or equally brief oral statements about a subject. On the other hand, there are topics or situations on which he wants very complete and very detailed information.

The staff has learned to time these longer memoranda so they will hit his night table. "He loves to have them then," said George Reedy. "He soaks them up. And he also has no hesitation about getting any of us on the phone at two A.M., if some point isn't clear."

The President has no real hobbies, unless it is winning at politics. He and a few Texas pals play a savagely vicious game of dominoes when Johnson finds the time, which isn't often. One of his favorite opponents was his longtime friend and aide, Walter Jenkins, until the latter's resignation during the presidential election campaign. The President will sit in a poker game for small stakes, but plays it indifferently and with little interest. He does not play bridge, despite stories to the contrary. Mrs. Johnson did teach him Canasta. He drinks occasionally but rarely until after dinner and then limits himself to Scotch and soda. He prefers Cutty Sark Scotch and the soda must always be from a fresh bottle.

The President's office in the West Wing of the White House is the same large, rounded room used by his predecessor. From his big desk he can, if he likes, step through French doors into the West Garden. There are bookcases on the walls and a number of chairs, including a rocker. Two divans, flanking a coffee table, are the scene of many of the more intimate conferences. One entrance opens on a main corridor but all visitors are ushered in through the secretary's office on the President's right, when he is at his desk.

With the exception of Timothy J. Reardon, Theodore C. Sorensen, Pierre Salinger and Arthur Schlesinger, Jr., the hard core of the John F. Kennedy "Irish Mafia" headed the President's urgent appeal and remained on the job through the 1964 presidential election.

Sorensen, who was Special Counsel and chief speech writer for President Kennedy, and Schlesinger, who worked on both United Nations and Latin American affairs (as well as on speeches) both resigned to write books on the late John F. Kennedy. Salinger, a Californian and one of the Mafia by adoption, left to run for the Senate from his home state. When the incumbent, Senator Clair Engle, died, Salinger was appointed by the California Governor to fill out the remaining months of Engle's term. In the election in November, Salinger was defeated.

The staff of any President inevitably reflects the character of the chief executive, plus the working habits he has picked up over his years in either public or private life, or both. Under Kennedy the tight little group of White House intimates exerted much greater political power collectively, and in some cases individually, than any of the cabinet members. The Johnson staff emerges more as a group of true assistants, reflecting both the caliber of selection and character of the President. He and he alone makes both the policies and the decisions.

(When Lyndon Johnson first ascended to the Presidency the man he leaned on most heavily and who became the closest thing to a chief of staff was Walter Jenkins, the close family friend who resigned under the cloud of a morals charge during the campaign. Jenkins had been Johnson's Administrative Assistant in the Senate and from long association knew how Johnson thought and how he reacted. In the early scrambling for position on the new White House staff, Jenkins floated close to the top without much effort, possibly because he had been Johnson's right hand for so long it had become habitual.)

The White House staff with which Johnson started his first elected term was announced from his Texas ranch late in January, 1965, after the Inauguration. It was a combination of the old and the new.

McGeorge Bundy remained as special assistant for national security affairs.

Lawrence F. O'Brien remained also, as assistant for Congressional Relations, but was expected to leave to collaborate on a book about John F. Kennedy as a politician.

George E. Reedy, who, like Jenkins, had been with Johnson for years as a labor expert and general handyman, had moved into the spot as Press Secretary vacated by Pierre Salinger. He remained there, until July, 1965, when he resigned for reasons of health.

Bill Don Moyers, who took over Jenkins' desk when he resigned and some of his aura of leadership, became Press Secretary when Reedy resigned.

Jack J. Valenti continued as appointments secretary; Horace Busby, cabinet secretary; Richard N. Goodwin, urban affairs and conservation; Douglass Cater, education and international affairs, while Lee C. White was promoted to Special Counsel.

W. Marvin Watson, formerly Texas State Democratic Chairman and assistant to the president of Lone Star Steel Company, was added to the staff after Johnson's original announcement.

Bundy, O'Brien, Goodwin and White, former members of the Kennedy staff, have fitted (or allowed themselves to be fitted) into the new regime with its distinctly Texas flavor.

Press Secretary Moyers, like Busby, Watson and Valenti, is a Texan and the youngest member of the staff. A former deputy director of the Peace Corps, he is from a little town near Fort Worth where he was an ordained Baptist minister.

Valenti is from Houston, an advertising and public relations executive. He is never far from the President during his waking hours and can find a memo or make a phone call almost as quickly as the President himself. He probably sees the President more than any other staff member and competes with Moyers and Bundy for staff prominence. Busby is a former Texas newsman. Douglass Cater, an Alabaman, is a Washington magazine writer and author.

The men and women who work for Lyndon Johnson are bound to him with a clear loyalty, although whether this loyalty is to the man or to his success might be difficult to determine at times. He is the most demanding of masters to serve. Life is neither easy nor placid on Johnson's staff. It is tough. He wants instant action, infinite attention to detail, perfection—and success.

Lyndon Johnson is essentially a man who understands and appreciates pure facts. He is not aware of their rationale. He is not interested in their hypothesis. His attention is caught by the fact itself. Given this solid actuality, he will hold it and examine it, feeling every contour, sensing every light and shadow. It is a concrete thing which may be useful and he is conscious of it in its most basic form.

He does not complicate his thoughts nor clutter his mind with abstractions.

The Johnson temper is notorious. He can, and frequently does, rail and storm at a staff member when their opinions cross.

"If you are right," said a long-time associate, "stand up to him. He will respect you for it. If you don't, you'll find yourself relegated to carrying the baggage."

2

☆

Young Lyndon in Texas

Twelve miles out of Johnson City, Texas, back a hundred yards or so from the Pedernales River and among a clump of twisted native live oak trees, is the spot where Lyndon Baines Johnson was born on August 27, 1908.

Some three-quarters of a mile up the river is the LBJ ranch house, the present "heart's home" of the President, his Texas residence. The ranch house has an air of gracious living. The setting, with its view of the quiet Pedernales, its grove of trees, the carpet grass lawn, swimming pool, stock barns, private landing strip and hangar, is beautiful and impressive.

The Johnson birthplace was none of these. The house there now was built from the rough planking of the house in which the President was born. It has three rooms, each perhaps twelve feet square. A screened porch on the front, boarded up half its height, completes the box. This house is unused today.

The original house, from photographs, was also three-roomed but more typical of early Texas farm homes. A forerunner of today's "breezeway" separated the kitchen from the living and sleeping quarters. There was a big stone fireplace. A roofed veranda stretched along the front. It may have afforded a view of the Pedernales River; the present house does not.

There is an air of abandonment about the place today. The door of an ancient backhouse, a "two-holer," sags open on rusty hinges. Cattle graze in the adjoining fields. The original Johnson farm was settled by Lyndon's grandfather in 1889. He also probably built the original house. The President's father, Sam Ealy Johnson, took his bride here in August, 1907, one year before Lyndon was born.

A few yards in front and to the side of the old house is the Johnson family cemetery, where the President's parents and grandparents are buried. The walled-in area is pleasant, among live oak trees that are estimated to be from four to five hundred years old.

Lyndon Johnson's first fifteen years were spent on this farm and in Johnson City, where the family moved from time to time to accommodate the elder Johnson's activities as a cotton trader, legislator and rancher. The town had been named for Lyndon's paternal grandfather, Sam Ealy Johnson, Sr., and his brother (Lyndon's great uncle), Tom Johnson, who settled there after the Civil War to raise cattle and drive them over the trails to Kansas.

One of Lyndon's schoolmates remembers the Johnson family as being terribly poor. Actually, in terms of the time, they were not. They lived on a scale normal to the community. There was always a roof overhead, food on the table, decent clothes and at least one pair of shoes around. The Johnson family, for three generations, was famous for its openhanded hospitality and ready welcome to visitors. Lyndon had a pony to ride from the farm to school.

Cash money was, of course, scarce, and there was little of it for extras. Throughout all of his boyhood, Lyndon earned his own spending money and he had a notable youthful career at finding odd jobs to pick up a nickel or a dime. Later, of course, he worked his way through college.

Mrs. J. B. Leonard, the gracious lady who is now the superintendent of schools in Johnson City, grew up with Lyndon Johnson. She was completely at ease dropping back some four decades to recall the way of life in the town when she, Lyndon and their schoolmates shared it.

Johnson City had, perhaps, some three hundred residents. Then, as now, it was a cross-roads town (Main Street and Nugent Avenue). There were no paved streets or roads. There was no electricity, no gas, a few telephones and a few automobiles. Johnson City had no trains and all supplies were brought in by mule cart.

"Lyndon was just one of the boys," Mrs. Leonard said. "He was well liked and always in on everything.

"We used to play baseball after supper. Usually there wouldn't be enough boys to make up two 'sides,' so they let the girls play, too. Supper was early and, in the summertime, it would be light quite late. If there was a moon, we played in the moonlight.

"In school the boys (and girls) played volleyball, basketball and baseball, and we had a track team. Every year there was a county field meet."

Mrs. Leonard didn't remember Lyndon's prowess as an athlete, but "the schools were so small and there were so few boys—everybody played."

The boys shot and trapped wild game. There were lots of squirrels and they made a welcome meat addition to the table fare, either fried or stewed with dumplings. The boys also hunted "varmints"—raccoons and foxes—always at night and with dogs. Later they were guided by auto headlights. Sometimes they would walk ten or twelve miles, searching out quarry.

They also ran trap lines for foxes and raccoons, to secure their pelts, with varying success. The whole school dreaded the days when any of the young trappers would catch and skin a skunk and come to school in grinning, odorous triumph!

"The ice cream parlor, of course, was the center of our social life," said Mrs. Leonard. "You met your friends there. There wasn't much 'dating' as such. Boys and girls paired off, but there was more group activity.

"We used to have parties in the homes Friday and Saturday nights. And, I think the parents took more of an interest in the activities of their children in those days. There were lots of family picnics and big family excursions to the river."

Outside of Johnson City a highway bridge crossed the Pedernales River, which formed a pleasant and not too deep pool at that point.

"It was where the Baptist Church took the converts for baptizing," continued Mrs. Leonard, "and it got to be known as the 'Baptizing Hole.' It was also the place where the boys went swimming."

The boys, Mrs. Leonard surmises, preferred to swim in the raw, but sometimes the girls would invade the Baptizing Hole, forcing the boys into swim suits.

"The girls didn't swim much," said Mrs. Leonard. "If

you will remember, we had to wear costumes down to our knees, stockings and bathing shoes. Anything less was disgraceful!"

Mrs. Leonard, and other friends, remember life in the Johnson home in Johnson City. The house, since remodeled, had two bedrooms, a living-dining room, kitchen and big screened-in back porch where the children slept. There was a great wood-burning fireplace in the living room and much of the family cooking was done here. There was always a pot of pinto beans suspended from a metal arm in the fireplace. Mrs. Leonard also remembers the toothsome sweet potatoes Lyndon's mother used to bake in a large iron skillet placed on the coals, with more coals heaped on the iron lid.

Cornbread was, of course, staple diet, along with bacon fried on the big wood-burning cookstove in the kitchen. These were supplemented by hominy grits, turnip greens and boiled beef.

There were movies in the Opera House, located on the second floor of the firehouse, on Friday and Saturday nights. Admission was fifteen cents to see William S. Hart, forerunner of all the Western stars, for Mary Pickford, Charlie Chaplin, William Farnum, Mae Marsh, Theda Bara, Wally Reid and other great performers of the silent screen days.

Lyndon earned his way into the movies by passing out handbills advertising the performances. He also spaded and raked gardens and did other outdoor chores to make money. In the summer, he and other town boys worked on the nearby ranches and farms. At that time some of the farmers around Johnson City raised cotton (no longer considered a worthwhile crop) and Lyndon, along with other schoolmates, girls as well as boys, considered it a great lark to go out in a gang and pick cotton, back-breaking work though it was. There was one barbershop in Johnson City and its shoeshine stand was a coveted concession among the high school boys. Lyndon got it.

In spite of Lyndon's farm background, the friends who knew him while he was growing up in Johnson City think of him as a town boy rather than a country boy. He was considered a neat dresser. A picture taken of the ninth, tenth and eleventh grades (as far as Johnson City high school went in those days) shows him as the only boy wearing a necktie, along with the superintendent and principal. He went with the "crowd" to the summer fairs in Fredericksburg. It was thirty miles from Johnson City, a two-and-a-half-hour trip, bumping over dirt roads in the automobiles of the day.

Lyndon was normally mischievous. A schoolmate remembers that the school superintendent used to date a pretty teacher. Interested in techniques, Lyndon and a group of friends piled boxes under the window of the girl's parlor and climbed up on their precarious perch to observe what went on. Apparently it wasn't very much because the narrator of the tale couldn't recall what they saw.

Lyndon Johnson graduated from high school in Johnson City in the late spring of 1924, when he was fifteen years old, over six feet tall and thin as a willow fishing pole. His grades had been both excellent and average, depending on his interest in the subject. His mother, Rebekah Baines Johnson, had been a large factor in the application of her son to his books. Mrs. Johnson was a private teacher of "elocution," as public declaiming was known at that time, and she taught Lyndon to read and to memorize and recite small poems before he was five. Later, she worked with him over his lessons and saw that he didn't get through the front gate on the way to school without knowing them. Sometimes this meant walking to the gate with him, reading the lesson aloud as they walked.

Graduation from high school was a release from drudgery for the young Texan, and, with a newly-acquired sense of freedom, he organized a group of like-minded friends and they struck out for California.

In *The Lyndon Johnson Story,* Booth Mooney says: "It might have been called 'running away.'" He quotes the President as remembering:

"'That was the first time I went on a diet. Nothing to eat was the principal item on my food chart. Up and down the coast I tramped, washing dishes, waiting on tables, doing farmwork when it was available, and always growing thinner and more homesick.'"

After some months of discovering that picking oranges wasn't as glamorous as it sounded, Johnson worked and hitchhiked his way back to Texas, very happy to be once more in a place where food came to the table in ample quantities three times a day.

The discomforts of living off the land in California had brought young Lyndon home, but they hadn't wrought any great changes in his totally disinterested attitude about higher education. For the next several months he worked at odd employment around the Johnson City community, ending with a job on a road gang.

This, for a boy of sixteen and seventeen, was back-breaking labor. Much of the time he was working with a "fresno," or dirt scraper. A fresno is a two-handled (or sometimes only one) metal scoop with a bail or hoop extending in front to which some kind of power is attached. In Lyndon Johnson's case, the power was a team of frequently irascible mules.

As operator of the fresno, Lyndon would stand behind the scraper and between the handles, one hand on each. The reins leading to the mules would be tied together and tightly stretched around his back, or perhaps over one shoulder and under one arm.

At the properly worded commands, the mules would drag the fresno along the ground. In the meantime, Lyndon would depress the handles so the front lip of the scraper would ride free. At precisely the right spot and moment, where loose dirt lay ready to be scraped up, the young driver would raise the handles just enough to let the lip bite in at the proper angle. Raised too little, the scraper would not get a load. Raised too much, the lip would strike hard ground and the mules would either stall or pull the scraper over.

Once he had a full load, Lyndon would again depress the handles and the scraper would ride over the ground to the dumping place. Then he would raise both handles in a great heave and, with the leverage from the mules, dump the load.

It was a job which required an understanding of mules, a strong back and the well-timed co-ordination of all concerned.

One day Lyndon arrived home, bone-weary from his work with the road gang, and fell on his bed. His mother came and sat beside him. She pointed out to him that his father had served five terms in the Texas legislature; that his grandfather had served one term as legislator and had also been Secretary of State for Texas. She reminded him that she, herself, was the great-niece of a man who had fought in the battle of San Jacinto, which won Texas freedom from Mexico. He had also signed the Declaration of Texas Independence and was a member of the first Congress of the Republic of Texas.

She might have gone further. Lyndon Johnson's forebears also include a governor of Kentucky, a co-founder of the Daughters of the American Revolution. His ancestors were of the pioneer stock of planters, lawyers, doctors and ministers who settled the states of the South—Kentucky, Georgia, Louisiana, Tennessee and North Carolina, as well as Texas.

She told him that both she and her father considered manual labor to be honorable. The time had come for him to decide whether he wanted that for the rest of his life or would rather work with his brains as well. If the latter should be the case, then he must consider further education.

Whether it was on account of the mules, the fresno, or his mother's persuasion, we are not sure, but Lyndon Johnson decided on education. Probably it was a combination of the three. He told his mother he would like to go to college. She called the Southwest State Teachers College, in San Marcos, Texas, that night and Lyndon entered college in the February term, 1927. He borrowed seventy-five dollars from the Johnson City Bank to pay his tuition, and got a job as school janitor to help defray other expenses.

Willard Deason, who now bosses KVET radio station in Austin, was a classmate and sometimes roommate of Lyndon Johnson at Southwest Teachers.

"It took Lyndon just about thirty days, I would say, to work his way out of that janitor's job," said Deason. "You know he wouldn't be a janitor very long. He got a better job, sort of second secretary in the college president's office. It paid more."

The youngster from Johnson City majored in history and also took English, economics and the usual math and science requirements. As in high school, his grades ranged from excellent to average, or even bad, if you want to include physical education, which he flunked.

Southwest Teachers was co-educational and most of the students lived and ate in boardinghouses. There were no dormitories. Lyndon stayed for a while in the Pirtle house, where Willard Deason was his roommate. Mrs. Pirtle was the widow of a San Marcos doctor and set a good table, Deason recalls, plain Southwest fare—grits, hot biscuits, stew and meat loaf. There was cereal for breakfast, and sometimes bacon and eggs.

Although he never held an elective office on the campus, Lyndon was tirelessly active as a behind-the-scenes manipulator of campus politics. After a few months at the college, he learned that the student offices were all controlled by a small group of athletic heroes who called themselves the "Black Stars." Finding a ready-made political organization, Lyndon decided to join it. He tried out as pitcher of the college baseball team, failed to make the grade and was blackballed by the Black Stars.

"So Lyndon organized the White Stars," said Deason. "There were nine members. The membership was very, very secret—just like that of the Black Stars. I was put up to be president of the student body.

"Actually, there were three different factions on the campus—the Black Stars, the White Stars and the Independents, sometimes known as the YMCA group.

"The night before election we of the White Stars held a caucus and decided we were beaten. After mourning over the fact for a while, everyone went home—everyone, that is, but Lyndon. He got on the phone and started calling the boardinghouses. He worked on the independent vote till four in the morning—and I won by eight ballots."

Southwest Teachers at that time had four semesters of three months each and student officers were elected for one term only.

"The Black Stars cut me to ribbons with every political maneuver and rumor they could think of for the next three months," remembers Deason. "We let them go right ahead, and then put up Albert Hartzke—he was popular—for the next term and he was elected. No one even knew Al was a White Star, but he was."

While Lyndon was content to let others hold elected offices, he did not neglect all campus distinctions. He edited the weekly *College Star*—that job paid thirty dollars a month—was a member of the Literary Society, President of the College Press Club, Secretary of the Schoolmasters Club and headed the debate team.

It is as a debater, as well as politician, that Lyndon is most remembered at Southwest Teachers. Reverend Elmer Graham, pastor of Lovera Boulevard Baptist Church in San Antonio, was his debate partner. The minister usually opened the debates and Lyndon closed them. He proved himself an artist at picking weak spots in the opposition arguments—a trait he developed to a high degree as the years went by.

From San Marcos, Lyndon wrote home: "Mother, I am now learning the things you have been trying to teach me since I was a little boy."

Lyndon Baines Johnson was graduated from Southwest State Teachers College in the spring of 1930 with a Bachelor of Science Degree, only three years and some months after entering, with a year of that period out for teaching in Cotulla, Texas. He accomplished this feat by attending college all four semesters and by taking extra courses.

About halfway between San Antonio and Laredo, on Highway 81, which connects at the border with the international roadway to Mexico, lies the town of Cotulla, Texas. Formerly it was two towns divided by a railroad track, Cotulla and LaSalle.

In 1929, when Lyndon Johnson, then twenty-one, went there as a teacher for one hundred dollars a month, to earn enough money to continue his own college education, the population of Cotulla totaled about three thousand persons. The place drew trade from the surrounding countryside and from occasional tourists en route to Mexico. This was ranching country and many of the ranchers would move into town for the winter or for the school term.

The Welhausen School, where Lyndon taught, was on the old LaSalle side of town and had been established the year before to accommodate the Mexican-Americans who lived there. The pupils had to be taught English before they could be taught other things. LaSalle was entirely Mexican-American, with three exceptions. Sheriff T. H. ("Chuc") Poole, Judge Covey Thomas, and Mrs. Mary Ida Reed all had homes there.

Dorothy Jackson, the granddaughter of Mrs. Reed, was fourteen when Lyndon Johnson came to Cotulla. At that time, she went to the other Cotulla school and was not particularly interested in the young teacher, but, later she became his secretary in Washington, where she met her husband, and later worked for his top aide in the White House.

"I was in Cotulla High School," said Mrs. Nichols, "and the President taught the fifth, sixth and seventh grades at Welhausen Grade School. But everyone in town knew him. He was tall and thin and completely full of energy. In addition to teaching at Welhausen, he also took on the job of coaching basketball at the high school. I remember that he would come there to coach the boys and if they weren't ready for him, he would coach the girls' softball team. Even then he couldn't bear to waste time."

Dorothy Jackson Nichols also remembers that Lyndon Johnson told her she wasn't a good enough player to make the team, an incident which rankled for some time.

The President roomed and boarded with Miss Sarah Tinsley, sharing a room with a high school football coach. This house, like other better residences of Cotulla, stood on poles or stilts, a few feet above the ground.

"Cotulla," explained Mrs. Nichols, "is termite country. Any wood in or on the ground is target for attack." So, the better houses were built on stilts, which could be replaced easily whenever necessary. Most of the Cotulla families kept chickens. They roosted, nested and dust-bathed under the stilt dwellings. However, many of the houses in which the Texas-Mexican families lived rested right on the ground, with the clean-swept earth serving as the floor. These poorer homes were invariably colorful, with the gay flowers that bloomed in the surrounding gardens as well as in window boxes.

"Cotulla was a quiet town," recalled Mrs. Nichols. "Things got pretty dead after supper. There was, and still is, just one movie house. The gay spot of the day came at four-thirty in the afternoon, when all of us dressed up and drove to the drugstore. There was curb service and we sat in cars and drank Cokes or sodas and traded gossip. Even in those days, no one in Texas ever *walked* anywhere."

The big meal of the day in Cotulla was dinner at noon and the staple dish was frijole beans.

"Everyone had frijoles," said Mrs. Nichols. "You put them on to cook at nine in the morning, so they would be ready. For supper, we usually just ate the leftovers from dinner."

Lyndon Johnson's former pupils, now approaching middle age, remember him as being strict but popular. He made them speak English on the playground, as well as in the classroom. Danny Garcia, now a prosperous furniture merchant of Cotulla, appeared on a nation-wide television program to tell how Johnson spanked him for misbehaving in class. Garcia was invited to the White House afterward and chatted with the President. He told reporters:

"The three grades the President taught were combined. There were about thirty of us. He used to leave us in class on our honor. One day I got up in front of the room and was clowning around. The President came tiptoeing back in. He took me by the hand and led me into his office. I thought I was going to get a lecture, but that wasn't it. He turned me over his knee and whacked me a dozen times on the backside."

Garcia, who was thirteen at the time, still "treasures the memory," he declares.

The school had little or no athletic equipment. The

President bought baseball and basketball gear for the children with money from his own pocket.

Lyndon took one boy who wasn't making the grade in his studies to Johnson City over a holiday in order to tutor him. The boy passed.

The big events in Cotulla were the Courthouse dances and the fiestas, held on the Mexican holidays of *Cinco de Mayo* and *Diez y Seis Septembre* (May 5 and September 16).

"The dances were held in the courtroom of the LaSalle County Courthouse, in Cotulla," said Dorothy Nichols. "Everyone went. Parents took their children. Every girl had her 'courthouse dress.' The older women wore long evening gowns, usually velvet, and real jewelry.

"The band was imported from San Antonio. We danced fox trots and waltzes. It was still the day of the flapper and the toddle was popular.

"All of the men wore ranch clothes—clean khakis—and cowboy boots. They would sneak out to their parked cars for a nip of whisky occasionally. There would always be one or two who got too much and were talked about for the next few months," Mrs. Nichols recalls.

"The President came to the dances—the whole town did. And we all went to the fiestas, which were held on the plaza in LaSalle. There were carnival games and stalls with handiwork from Mexico. The music would be local—usually guitar—and only the neighborhood girls and boys danced. The girls sat in chairs around the dance area. Their mammas stood behind them. When a boy came up and asked for a dance, the girl got a yes or no signal from her mamma."

At the end of the school term in Cotulla, Lyndon Johnson returned to college at San Marcos. He graduated the following summer. After teaching debating and public speaking for a year at the Sam Houston High School in Houston, he went to Washington to begin a career in politics.

3

☆

The Texan Goes to Washington

The year 1932 saw the United States in the depths of its greatest depression. It was a time of bread lines and soup kitchens. Men sold apples on the street corners and the phrase, "Brother can you spare a dime," became a part of the language, as well as the title of a musical hit.

This depressed 1932 was also the year Lyndon Johnson came to Washington to begin an apprenticeship in the fine art of politics and to start a career which has carried him to the nation's highest office. He came as secretary to Richard Kleberg, who had been elected to the House of Representatives from the 14th District of Texas in a special election in November, 1931.

Dick Kleberg was a product of the world's largest land holding, the King Ranch, which lies in southwest Texas, between Corpus Christi and Brownsville, at the Mexican border. Starting in pre-Civil War times with a few acres, named the Santa Gertrudis, the King and Kleberg families (the King daughter married a Kleberg) extended the ranch boundaries to its present million-plus acres, grazing close to a million head of cattle. The state of Connecticut could be dropped within the King Ranch and not touch a fence. On it was produced the Santa Gertrudis breed of cattle, a cross between the shorthorn and the Brahma. The King Ranch racing stable has bred a Kentucky Derby winner. The ranch staffs its own successful agricultural experiment station. Richard Kleberg was one of the heirs to the King Ranch and lived there.

Lyndon Johnson had taken a post teaching in the Sam Houston High School, in Houston, Texas, after his graduation from college. There he had taught public speaking and debate, the things he himself had excelled at during his college days. The high school debating team he coached was notably successful, coming within one point of winning the state championship.

Politics, however, was inbred in the lives of the Johnson and the Baines families and Lyndon accepted his inheritance with no real reluctance. Added to his own inclinations was, it seems likely, the influence of two family friends: Sam Rayburn, who served with Lyndon's father in the Texas legislature and went on to the United States House of Representatives, and Roy Miller, one-time mayor of Corpus Christi and an immensely popular Washington lobbyist for the Texas Gulf Sulphur Co. Both knew Kleberg, of course, and Miller in particular was a close friend. And both knew and liked Lyndon.

Johnson worked for Kleberg during his election. He made speeches and he rang doorbells in personal solicitation for votes. More, he organized other workers in an early display of the talent he later developed to its highest degree. When Kleberg was elected, he asked Lyndon to be his legislative secretary and the young man was glad to accept.

It would have been difficult to find two men more differing in backgrounds. Richard Kleberg had never had to think seriously about the need for money; Lyndon had thought about it seriously most of his life. Kleberg had been born on the King Ranch, where the front gate was twenty miles from the ranchhouse—a spacious, lovely home. Lyndon was born in a three-room farmhouse on the Pedernales River, where his mother's butter and egg money was an important part of the family's living. Kleberg's friends and associates were, like himself, wealthy and conservative. Kleberg listened to, respected and agreed with their point of view. It is doubtful if Lyndon Johnson at that time would have thought of himself as a liberal; even then in much of Texas the term was almost synonymous with socialist. He did know that many of Dick Kleberg's farming and ranching constituents needed help, although his ideas must have been vague as to how this help could be achieved.

Herbert Hoover was President when Lyndon Johnson arrived in Washington, to discover a life that was new and different, and wider even than his beloved Texas. The Republicans still controlled the Senate but the Democrats had a small majority in the House and were already tasting victory in the autumn. It was evidently time for a change.

Washington is always a city where politics rules the conversation as well as the maneuvering. Johnson found the political air of Capitol Hill charged with the impendence of the approaching election and he was caught up with an excitement he has never lost.

Booth Mooney, in his book *The Lyndon Johnson Story,*

relates an observation on the young Texan's first days in Washington. He writes:

> Arthur Perry, at that time Secretary to Senator Tom Connally of Texas and already well versed in the ways of Capitol Hill, recalled the impact the newcomer made on the group of established secretaries.
>
> "I remember when Dick Kleberg brought Lyndon around to our office and told me he wished I would show him the way around Washington," Perry said. "Lyndon started asking questions as soon as he knew my name. He followed the same procedure with everyone else he met. He was out to learn all he could and learn it fast.
>
> "You never had to tell him anything a second time," said Perry. "This skinny boy was as green as anybody could be, but within a few months he knew how to operate in Washington better than some who had been here for twenty years before him."

Lyndon, along with many of the Capitol Hill aides and even some of the young, unmarried legislators, lived in the Dodge Hotel on Capitol Plaza. The hotel, originally the Grace Dodge, had been established as a hostel for working women, but, with the depression, its two lower floors had been partially opened to men.

These floors were below the lobby level, but, since the building was constructed with the slope of the land, they had windows at side and rear. Floor "B," immediately below the ground level, was made up of double rooms with connecting baths. Floor "A," another story down, had double rooms also, but the baths were at the ends of the hall.

The Dodge management divided Floor "B" and permitted men in one half, as well as in all of Floor "A." Two men occupied each room, and seniority of occupancy ruled the choice of location. The price per month was the same for all—$40.00 a room, $20.00 a man—for each room. The price included daily maid service. Representative Maury Maverick of San Antonio, Texas, lived on the "A" floor for several months.

The usual working hours on Capitol Hill in those days were from nine in the morning until four-thirty in the afternoon and it was completely normal that the staff assistants who toiled together during the day should continue the association after working hours.

They did. Walking to and from their offices, at meals and sitting around the practically dormitory rooms of the Dodge, they debated and argued endlessly about the legislation in both houses, its merits and chances of passing; about their Congressional employers, how they would vote and what were their chances for re-election; about the political policies of both parties.

Johnson was usually the catalyst. He would toss a subject into the maelstrom of debate and listen to all sides. Often he would interpose arguments, but his friends learned that he would take just about any point of view to bring out more opinions and more facts. His search for information and ideas was unending.

In the fall of 1934, Johnson's thirst for knowledge, plus a probable observation that, in legislative backgrounds, legal training led all the rest, sent him to Georgetown University, where he enrolled in night law school.

He had, by this time, brought up two of his prize debaters from Sam Houston High School, where he had taught, and had put them to work with him in Kleberg's office. Their dual purpose in venturing to Washington was employment and an education in law.

Luther E. Jones, now a lawyer in Corpus Christi, enrolled at Georgetown with Johnson. Gene Lattimer, now with the Civil Defense organization at Dennison, Texas, attended Washington College at Law.

Enrolling at Georgetown at the same time was Russell Morton Brown, now senior partner in his Washington law firm. The odds of seating arrangements put Brown next to Johnson in class and started a friendship which has lasted through many years and political campaigns.

"I didn't have enough money to buy books," said Brown, "so I studied at the Library of Congress—when I wasn't out pounding the streets, looking for a job. Father Francis Lucey, the Regent, let me—and a lot of other boys in those days—go to school on tick.

"When Lyndon found out I didn't have any money, he told me to come to Kleberg's office and he would put me to work there. But there wasn't much money available around there, either, so Lyndon got me a job over at Agriculture."

With money in his jeans, Brown moved into the Dodge Hotel, along with the others. In those depression days, $25.00 a week was considered a good salary for any but the better jobs, and no one had very much loose money. Johnson, with a Congressional secretary's salary of $3,000, annually was better off than many of the others.

"But Lyndon sent part of his pay check home," said Brown, "and then he always seemed to be loaning or giving money to someone. Once we all saw notices of a sale at Grossner's. This was a store between 13th and 14th, on F Street. They were advertising suits for sale cheap.

"Lyndon said: 'Russ, go down and get yourself a suit.' I guess he thought I needed one. I said, 'Hell, Lyndon, I haven't got any money to buy a suit. The rent's due.'

"Lyndon told me to go on down and charge a suit to his account, and I did. A few months later, he asked me if I had the suit paid for yet. I told him there was one more payment due on it. He said to let him know when it was paid for; he wanted to buy one."

The Dodge Hotel at that time had a good restaurant, but meals there, Brown remembers, cost a dollar. So the Johnson crowd usually went across Capitol Plaza to the All States Restaurant.

"It had plaques of the seals of all the states up on the walls and was quite a tourist attraction," Brown said, "but we went there for what the Texas boys called 'Fo bitters'— all you could eat for fifty cents. Just before paydays we used to eat at Childs, where you could do pretty well on two bits."

Because of Kleberg's fondness for golf, Johnson functioned in the Texas Representative's office with considerably more responsibility and authority than most Congressional secretaries. Dick Kleberg would answer roll call every day and he was usually present for important votes, but, according to many recollections of the time, he spent a fair share of his days at the Burning Tree Country Club.

Johnson was, in effect, office manager and, on some occasions, the voice of his employer's conscience. He passed out assignments to the staff workers, read and checked the temper of the mail, answered correspondence, received callers, studied the Congressional Record and maintained the necessary liaison activities with both other secretaries and Congressmen.

One important piece of legislation of the early New Deal days under newly-elected President Roosevelt was the

Triple A—the Agricultural Adjustment Act. It was a controversial measure, both in its enactment and its enforcement. Among other things, it provided for the plowing under of crops and the destruction of livestock to reduce the nation's agricultural surplus. It was much discussed, both in Congress, in the press and throughout the country.

Kleberg planned to vote against the measure.

Learning of his decision, Johnson protested. He told Kleberg that, from reading the mail and talking to visitors, he felt Kleberg's constituents were for the bill; thought it would help them. The Congressman shook his head; his friends didn't like the legislation. He didn't like it.

Johnson spent the next two days analyzing and tabulating the mail from the 14th Texas District. He found the letters and telegrams were running some thirty to one in favor of enacting the Triple A measure.

He got on the telephone and polled the secretaries of other Congressmen—the "Little Congress" of Capitol Hill. From these friends and colleagues he learned that the bill would pass and by a considerable majority.

Johnson talked to Kleberg again. He told him about the mail and its preponderance in favor of passage of the bill.

"Mister Dick," he said, "these people are your constituents. They want that bill passed. You can't vote against it."

Kleberg said he could, and he would. "The bill," he said, "is socialistic."

"Then," said Johnson, "I quit. The people voted for you. They put you in office. You represent them. If you vote against this bill, you'll be letting them down and I don't want them to think I had anything to do with it.

"Besides," he added, playing the ace, "the bill is going to pass anyway. I've polled the House and I know it."

Kleberg gave in.

The story of Johnson's triumph in becoming Speaker of the Little Congress in his first year as a Congressional Secretary has been widely told, but should not have come as a surprise to anyone who knew him at college. In campus politics, he had wrested control from the "Black Stars" there by the same tactics—superlative organization.

The Little Congress was an organization of Congressional Secretaries, modeled in its operation after the House of Representatives. The top officer was the Speaker, and, as in the House, it was a spot normally reserved for one of the more senior secretaries.

Lyndon went to a few meetings and observed that they were sparsely attended and that he usually saw the same faces present. He learned that many secretaries had never bothered to join, particularly the newer men, and that many who did belong found the sessions uninspiring.

It was a situation made to order for the talents of Lyndon Johnson. Whether he was persuaded to run, as has been reported, or whether he precipitated the persuasion, is not a matter of record. The outcome was a foregone conclusion.

With the help of his ardently willing friends in the Dodge House basement, Lyndon worked the secretarial side of the House of Representatives like a precinct captain. Those men who didn't belong to the Little Congress were induced to become members, because by so doing they would be able to vote for Lyndon Johnson as Speaker. Those already members were prevailed upon to attend the election and to vote for Lyndon because he promised interesting, exciting meetings.

The Little Congress met in one of the House hearing

rooms. The night of the election it was packed. A new and
—to some—surprising name was put forward as a candidate
and when the smoke of balloting cleared away Lyndon
Johnson was the new Speaker by a comfortable majority.
Until it was all over the opposition didn't know what had
hit them.

Johnson lived up to his word in enlivening the sessions
of the Little Congress. He persuaded leading Representatives and Senators, as well as other important Washington
figures, to address them. One session which Russell Brown
remembers well was the night Senator Huey Long of
Louisiana spoke.

Senator Long was at this time at the high point in a
career which was quite high in itself. As governor, Long
had ruled Louisiana for years, well or otherwise, depending
on the point of view. He was a nationally-known figure
long before coming to Washington and on the floor of the
Senate he extended the Long variety of demagoguery even
more widely.

"This was about the time," Brown recalls, "that he was
saying he thought he would run against Roosevelt. He had
had, or at least he so reported to police, a number of bomb
scares. He said they were planted in his office—and they
may have been.

"The evening that the Senator was scheduled to speak
was just after one of those scares and the reporters and news
photographers got their first chance at him when he came
to the Little Congress meeting as speaker on Lyndon's program.

"The Senator had a way of throwing up one arm and
assuming an arresting pose," said Brown. "It was very effective with audiences. I remember that he had just taken this

position when a flash bulb exploded. Senator Long thought it was a bomb. The result was pure bedlam."

Both Russell Brown and Arthur Perry recall that Lyndon's social life, along with others of the Dodge Hotel clique, was limited.

"We used to have an occasional date, usually with the Congressional girl secretaries," said Brown, "and there were parties, of course. We never brought girls to the Dodge. It was strictly segregated and, even if we had succeeded in sneaking a girl in, there wouldn't have been any privacy."

The boys almost always went, Brown recalls, to the meetings of the Texas State Society.

"We called it the Texas Club. They would have dances and we usually went as a gang, sometimes with girls, sometimes not. Lyndon always went along but I don't think he ever went with any special girl. He was a good dancer, or at least the girls said so—and they thought he was handsome, too—but he usually danced with the wives of the Texas Congressmen, rather than with the single girls."

Arthur Perry remembers some of their other social activities, and Lyndon's participation.

"Living at the Dodge," he said, "was like living in a permanent debating society, with Lyndon as the focal point. We were always talking, always arguing. Once in a while we would go to a ball game. Lyndon would go along because he didn't want to be left behind, but he didn't give a hoot about the game. He would keep right on arguing politics through every inning."

On one of his trips back to Texas, in September of 1934, Lyndon Johnson met Lady Bird Taylor in Austin. She was, perhaps, the first girl he had ever met who attracted him strongly. In Washington, he was simply too busy learning and living the political life of the nation's capital to bother with girls.

The First Lady was christened Claudia Alta Taylor. She has written concerning her nickname:

> When I was a baby, and in no position to protest, the family cook and maid-of-all-work gave me the nickname, Lady Bird, although I had the perfectly respectable calling name of Claudia. My parents and later my playmates took up the nickname and it stuck. At the age of thirteen, a most conventional time of life for girls, I tried to get rid of Lady Bird once and for all. I entered a new school and promptly announced all around that my name was Claudia. But old friends infiltrated and the first thing I knew, there it was again. Long ago I made peace with the nickname.

When Lyndon met Lady Bird it was different. He asked her for a date within a few minutes of the introduction, but she was returning to her home in Marshall, Texas, that evening, and Lyndon, of course, had to go back to Washington. The courtship was carried on by mail, telegram, long distance phone and a minimum of personal meetings.

"It was all typical of Lyndon," said Brown. "I didn't meet Bird until Lyndon brought her to Washington, but I'm sure he saw her, made up his mind he wanted to marry her and did. I don't think Bird ever had a chance to say no —if she wanted to."

Lady Bird and Lyndon were married on November 17, 1934, in St. Mark's Episcopal Church, in San Antonio. Dan Quill, a friend of Lyndon's and presently Postmaster of San Antonio, arranged details of the wedding and remembers the occasion very well.

"Lyndon called me from Texarkana on Friday," he related, "and said he and Lady Bird wanted to be married the next day in St. Mark's. Would I please arrange all the details.

"It wasn't exactly a question. In those days—in the group around Lyndon—you just called up and asked your friend to do something. You explained a few of the details and then hung up—kept out of touch. Friend was expected to carry on.

"I had a little trouble with the rector—Reverend Arthur R. McKinstry. He said he wasn't a justice of the peace; that he wanted his marriages to last. He wished to talk to the couple before he married them. He liked things more orderly.

"I was a member of the church and knew him pretty well, so I was able to talk him into it." Reverend McKinstry became a bishop later and is now retired.

Dan Quill also had a little trouble rounding up a small group for the wedding on such short notice, but finally, as he recalls now, he managed to collect some ten people. He found another Johnson friend, Henry Hirshberg, a Harvard graduate and San Antonio attorney. He proposed that Hirshberg be best man. Hirshberg thought Quill should be, but finally accepted the post. Mrs. Hirshberg also attended.

"Texarkana is four hundred miles from San Antonio," said Quill. "Lyndon had apparently driven from Washington and picked up Lady Bird at her home in Karnack, near Marshall, Texas. They didn't arrive, of course, until late Saturday afternoon.

"I hadn't done anything about a ring. They'd passed half a dozen towns with jewelry stores on the way but I guess they weren't thinking about such incidentals. At any rate, when they arrived—no ring.

"We were at the Plaza Hotel, where they stayed, and I went across the street to a store. I didn't know Lady Bird's size, of course, so I brought back half a dozen and Lady Bird found one that fit."

The store was Sears & Roebuck and the ring cost, Quill remembers, $2.50.

"I saw Lady Bird in Washington a few years ago," said Quill, "and asked her if she still had the ring. She does have it and said it was one of her most treasured possessions. She keeps it in her lockbox.

"The ceremony went off without incident. One of Lady Bird's University of Texas girl classmates stood up with her. Afterward, the wedding party walked across the Plaza from the church to the St. Anthony hotel for a wedding supper.

"We thought we should have a drink to celebrate," said Quill, "but we couldn't afford the St. Anthony prices on wine. Hirshberg remembered that he had a bottle at home and went after it. We had that to toast the bride and groom."

The couple went to Mexico City for their honeymoon. Rebekah Baines Johnson, Lyndon's mother, pasted in her scrapbook a snapshot of them taken in a flower-laden boat at the floating gardens of Xochmilco, a few miles out of the Mexican capital.

The Johnsons arrived in Washington with no special fanfare. Arthur Perry recalls that they spent their first night at least at the Dodge, presumably in one of the upper floor rooms. His first meeting with Lady Bird was at breakfast in the Dodge dining room. The Johnsons then moved into

an apartment they had subleased from friends on Connecticut Avenue. Later, they transferred to another apartment
on Columbia Road. Both of these early homes were in the
northwest section of Washington.

The Dodge gang missed the catalytic force of Lyndon
Johnson from their incessant debates, but the association
hardly broke up. His friends saw him on Capitol Hill during the days and were frequent guests at the Johnson apartment. Russell Brown recalls that the young couple had the
usual newly-wed problems of acquiring sufficient furniture.
There were blank spots in the decor.

Although she possibly didn't think of it as such then,
Lady Bird lost no time after arriving in preparing herself
to be a Washington politician's wife. This requires, among
other things, the ability to guide visiting friends, important
constituents and friends of important constituents around
the monuments, memorials and historic spots of Washington with a cheery smile. The smile is important, especially
when you've done it the third day in a row.

"Lady Bird would organize tours," said Russell Brown.
"She could never get Lyndon to go along—he always said
he was too busy—but she would organize the rest of us into
trips to Mount Vernon, the Lee Mansion, the Great Falls
of the Potomac or wherever she had in mind. I learned a
lot about Washington I hadn't known before."

The new Mrs. Johnson was a serious student of politics,
too, and of the ways of Washington life, which were as new
to her as they had been to Lyndon. She looked, learned and
profited. A friend once remarked that it would be hard to
overestimate the influence of two women on Lyndon Johnson's life—his mother and his wife.

"Lady Bird had just as much ambition as Lyndon," he

said. "It was always for Lyndon and she had it under better control."

Lyndon continued his studies at Georgetown Law School, attending the night classes until the end of the term, in the spring of 1935. His appointment as Texas Administrator of the National Youth Administration came in August of that year and, of course, ended his law studies. Russell Brown doubts that he would have continued in any case.

"The law," said Brown, "is essentially a clerical profession. Lyndon was impatient to do things. He always completed his homework, but when the professor would cover the same ground as the book, Lyndon would get restless. 'He's not telling me anything I don't know,' he would say. Lyndon certainly could have gone on and passed the bar had he wanted to, and he would have made a marvelous advocate—a courtroom lawyer. But he would never have had the patience to do the office work necessary to prepare a case."

Franklin D. Roosevelt, not only the man himself, but his beliefs and political philosophy, greatly influenced the life of Lyndon Johnson. In his 1937 campaign for Congress, Johnson successfully tied his political fortune to the New Deal. It was incidental that, in winning the election, he attracted the attention of FDR.

Long before that, when Johnson was a secretary in Kleberg's office, he had found the precepts of the New Deal and the temper of the men Roosevelt gathered about him greatly to his liking. For the first time, probably, he was able to crystallize his own thinking in terms of action by government. When he had argued with Kleberg that he must vote for the Triple A farm bill it was because he felt strongly that big government had the political power and the moral requirement to do something for the little man.

He had watched the nation lie mired in the depression for more than three years. The lack of money, the farm foreclosures, the bread lines were very real and close. Now he was looking at a tremendously enthusiastic program to put the country back on its feet and he liked what he saw. He felt that Roosevelt was the champion of the poor and the underprivileged and in so being, he became the Lyndon Johnson champion, too.

In one of the innumerable Dodge Hotel debates, Lyndon himself was the subject. One man said:

"Lyndon will go which way the wind blows."

And another added:

"Maybe, but if he does, he'll probably beat the wind there."

In the case of Johnson and Roosevelt, then and in later years, it was more likely a case of Johnson's being led along a course he inherently wanted to follow. Liberalism was not particularly involved, at least not in the sense it is known today. There is little doubt, though, that many of his present liberal convictions were formed in those early New Deal days, when the most he could do about them was apply well-adjusted thumbscrews to Richard Kleberg when he felt Mr. Dick's constituents were being outraged.

4

With the NYA
(National Youth Administration)

In 1933 there were five million unemployed youth in the
United States, and millions more faced the certainty of
dropping out of high school and college because their families could not afford to feed and clothe them, let alone pay
tuition where required.

Newly elected President Roosevelt first recognized this
youth problem by starting the Civilian Conservation Corps
soon after he assumed office. Then, on June 26, 1935 he
established the National Youth Administration by Executive Order. It read, in part:

"I have determined that we shall do something for the
nation's unemployed youth, because we can ill afford to
lose the skill and energy of these young men and women.
They must have their chances in school, their turn as ap-
prentices and their opportunity for jobs . . . a chance to
work and earn for themselves."

Divisions of the NYA were established in each state, with
a State Director to serve as the Executive Officer.

In August, 1935, just a few days before his twenty-seventh birthday, Lyndon Johnson was named State Director for Texas. He resigned his position as Secretary to Texas Congressman Richard Kleberg and flew immediately from Washington to Austin. At the airport he told reporters he thought his job was to work himself out of a job. He promptly went to Governor James Allred at the State Capital, presented his credentials and received assurances of co-operation. Most of that night he spent on the telephone, getting together the nucleus of an organization.

His first employee was Sherman Birdwell, now Texas State Employment Commissioner. (Another was Willard Deason, now head of KVET radio station in Austin and a former roommate in college as previously stated.) Birdwell was later to follow Johnson to Washington as his secretary in the House of Representatives.

The second man Johnson moved to corral was Jesse Kellam, at that time Deputy State Supervisor of Education. Kellam was a neighbor and friend from Blanco County. He had preceded Lyndon Johnson through college at San Marcos. The new NYA Director wanted Kellam as his deputy.

Approached, Kellam told Johnson that he had just been promoted and felt it would be unfair to his superiors to leave. Johnson asked if he would take a month's leave, if Johnson could contrive it. Kellam agreed. Johnson obtained the leave. Later, he had this extended to one year. When Johnson left Texas in 1937 to run for Congress, Kellam was still on the job and succeeded him as director. Kellam now manages Radio-TV Station KTBC in Austin. It is owned by the Johnson family.

In establishing NYA, President Roosevelt set out four major objectives for the new organization.

1. To provide funds for the part-time employment of needy school, college and graduate students so as to enable them to continue their education.

2. To provide funds for the part-time employment on work projects of young persons, the projects being designed primarily not only to give these young people valuable work experience, but to benefit youth generally in the local community.

3. To establish and to encourage the establishment of job training, counseling and placement services for youth.

4. To encourage the development and extension of constructive and job-qualifying leisure-time activities.

From its inauguration, the NYA was a two-pronged operation. One goal was to provide employment to keep boys and girls in school. The other was to get jobs for those who had already, to some degree or other, ended their education.

Three precepts were laid down for all work undertaken by the young people under NYA's supervision: 1) it must be useful and bona fide; 2) it must have a training value and 3) wages were to be paid for doing it.

From NYA's inception until its close in 1943, $166,838,-000 was disbursed nationally to more than 2,134,000 students to permit them to continue their education. Some $467,600,000 was paid for the work of 2,677,000 youngsters out of school.

The first offices of the Texas NYA consisted of four rooms on the sixth floor of the Littlefield Building in Austin. Furniture was "scrounged" from one of the state welfare agencies, phones were hooked up, the staff assembled and they went to work.

Lyndon Johnson's first move was to go to the Texas State Highway Department, an excellently organized and operating agency. To the highway engineer, he said:

"Roadside parks are popular and useful. You've got the land along the highways and the native lumber to work with. I've got the manpower. Let's get together."

As a result, fifteen thousand NYA boys cleared, drained and landscaped hundreds of park areas for motorists on the Texas highways, and built tables, benches and even stone barbecue pits for them. When this maneuver proved successful, Johnson went to other operating state agencies and tied his project in with theirs. Later, this co-operation even included the Fort Sam Houston Army Post, where 2,000 young men were employed.

As a consequence, the NYA in Texas was a going concern long before most of the other states, which usually attempted to form self-independent agencies, had any effective plan of procedure. Aubrey Williams, National Director of the NYA, frequently praised Lyndon Johnson's operation as outstanding and cited it as a model for other states.

Kellam, Birdwell and Deason all recall the frantic "organized" confusion of the early days of the organization. The office in Austin was woefully understaffed. The Director was busy night and day, scouring the state for district and county supervisors, instigating and approving projects.

The working hours in the Austin office mounted to sixteen and eighteen a day. The Littlefield Building had its own power plant and turned the lights off, normally, at midnight. Almost every night saw Johnson in the basement, begging the building superintendent to leave the power on for another hour or two.

Eighty-four colleges and junior colleges and over two hundred public schools had quickly qualified for NYA assistance under eligibility regulations which required them to be nonprofit, tax exempt and bona fide educational institutions holding day sessions.

The student aid worked with as little red tape as Johnson could manage. School officials, once their institutions were declared qualified, laid out the jobs, screened the students and determined the hours and earnings within limits prescribed from Austin.

Between seventy-five and one hundred thousand students were able to continue in Texas colleges because of NYA help. Seven hundred and fifty of these attended the University of Texas in the first year. The number totaled 7,500 throughout the entire program.

Willard Deason remembers the University of Texas dean walking into the NYA office one day with a sheaf of applications he had been forced to cut out because of the lack of funds allocated to him. There was never enough money.

"I feel like I have blood on my hands," he said.

The applications literally poured in, Deason and Kellam both remember. Every one had to be processed, judged and handled. The staff worked hours overtime, for which there was, of course, no compensation.

"Lyndon Johnson taught me the meaning of loyalty," said Sherman Birdwell. "He breeds it. It makes you want to do a job both you and he will be proud of. He made us all feel that way."

He remembers one midnight when Johnson walked through the office. One of the men sat there, almost in tears. His desk was piled high with applications and correspondence. The Director stopped.

"I'm answering a letter from the top of this stack," said the clerk. "And I know that further down in this pile is another letter from the same person, asking why I haven't replied to the original. There are dozens like that."

Johnson studied the man and the desk. "You're answering early letters off the top of the pile when you know there will be other letters down below which came later from the same persons?"

The clerk nodded.

Johnson reached down and turned the pile of correspondence over.

"Work from the bottom," he said. "That ought to cut the job just about in half."

Texas has, of course, large segments of both Negro and Texas-Mexican citizens among its population. In the NYA there was no segregation, no color barrier. White, Negro and Mexican-descended boys and girls worked together without difficulty.

Lyndon Johnson spent much of his time on the road, checking on his area and district supervisors and their projects, and sometimes making speeches. On one occasion he addressed a luncheon club in San Antonio. The group was a little too conservative to coincide with the ideas of a New Dealer like Johnson, and while he was chatting with members prior to speaking, one remarked that "All these kids need to do is get out and hustle."

"Right," said Johnson. "Last week over here I saw a couple of your local kids hustling—a boy and a girl, nine or ten. They were hustling through a garbage can in an alley."

Money for NYA, in the early days, came from the WPA

(Works Projects Administration) and usually was as much as Director Aubrey Williams could wangle. (Later NYA was financed by direct appropriation and also, the WPA became the Works Progress Administration.) No matter how much money Johnson was able to get, however, it was always too little by the time it was divided up among the state organizations, according to population.

As a consequence, money was doled out like the gold it represented. For children in public schools, the amount might be five or six dollars a month—enough for at least one hot meal a day. College youths were limited to thirty dollars a month.

"We made our money go a long way," remembers Deason. "Instead of giving one kid thirty, we gave two kids fifteen dollars each."

In the months directly after its beginning, the Texas NYA continued to develop projects and jobs, both for students and for boys and girls who had finished their schooling. At one point, 23,000 students were being aided by part-time work and 24,000 additional youth were given an opportunity to develop manual skills through the program.

Male students repaired, and constructed entirely, school buildings and libraries, gyms and dormitories, athletic fields, tennis courts, and swimming pools, as well as doing such minor chores as waiting tables, yard and lab work, and washing dishes. Girls served lunches in school cafeterias, made hospital supplies, sewed clothing, bound and restored books, helped in nursery schools.

The out-of-school young men were given jobs in a variety of shops—woodworking, foundry and sheet metal. They repaired radios, autos and electrical appliances. Girls were taught homemaking, cooking, cafeteria management, nursing fundamentals and how to prepare hospital meals.

At Kenedy, Texas, nine schoolboys remodeled two hundred old desks and put them back in service. At the San Diego (Texas) High School, boy students built a 24'x30' frame building to house a library and athletic equipment. At Baylor University, in Waco, ten young sociology majors visited and worked to reinstate "drop out" cases in the Waco public schools and achieved the remarkable record of one failure in 1,849 cases. The University of Texas hired high school boys all over the state to catch fruit flies for biology experiments.

In San Antonio, the square block devoted to Mexican art and craftwork, La Villita, was restored by NYA workers, as was an historic landmark, the former home of Mexican General Martín Perfecto de Cos, who surrendered to the Texans who fought and won independence from Mexico. The "Little Chapel in the Woods," at Texas State College for Women, in Denton, was built by both boys and girls of NYA, and dedicated on November 2, 1939, by Mrs. Eleanor Roosevelt.

Lyndon Johnson worked equally as strenuously as his staff to make the Texas NYA project the success it was. Mrs. Johnson joined him in Austin shortly after his appointment and the couple rented a house from friends. Birdwell recalls that many inpromptu staff meetings were held there over dinners cooked by the President's wife.

"Lady Bird was a good cook," he remembers. "She was especially good at cooking round steak, which was about all we could afford in those days. She was also the only person who could cook spinach so I would eat it."

He remembers too, driving into Austin with a group of NYA district supervisors after an inspection trip.

"It was way past noon and one of the men in the back seat whispered loudly wasn't it about time for lunch.

"Lyndon was driving. He wheeled the car into the next drive-in and told the girl carhop, 'Ten hamburgers and five bottles of milk.' That was our executive lunch."

All of Johnson's colleagues recall the watchful eye he kept over NYA projects—and workers. Many like to tell a related anecdote.

One day the State Director drove out to Brackinridge Park, in San Antonio, to look over a project there, designed to train young men and women as athletic and recreation leaders. He found the supervisor all alone.

"Where are the workers?" Johnson queried.

"They're due a little later," was the reply.

Johnson asked how many there were. The supervisor was vague. The Director drove back to the San Antonio office, had a few words with the District chief and returned to Austin.

After he had gone, the District man called the recreation supervisor on the phone and asked him if he had had any visitors lately.

"Yes," answered the supervisor. "There was a tall man named Johnson who came by. He seemed to speak with some authority."

"Yeah," said the District man. "He speaks with enough authority that your project is closed out—and you with it."

Early in 1937, after Lyndon Johnson had been Texas NYA Director some eighteen months, Representative James P. Buchanan, who represented Johnson's home district, died. A special election was called to choose a successor.

Johnson entered the race and, on his own judgment and that of some astute Texas political friends, decided to base his platform on the complete support of the Roosevelt New Deal program. He drew his savings from the bank and, with the addition of money his wife borrowed on property she had inherited, tossed his hat into what proved to be a crowded ring.

There were eight other candidates in the contest, all conservatives. Johnson said they were "I'm for Roosevelt, but . . ." men, and hung on them the term "the Eight in the Dark."

Not long before, President Roosevelt, angered because certain of his New Deal legislation was being judged unconstitutional by the Supreme Court, sought to increase the Court's membership to liberalize its decisions. The plan was widely known as the "Court packing proposal."

Johnson supported the Roosevelt plan entirely, the only one of the nine candidates who did, but always referred to it as the "unpacking plan" to get things accomplished. In a speech he made on March 18, 1937, at Austin, he said:

"I want to make one thing clear. The main plank in my platform is the support of President Roosevelt and his administration. And that includes his position on the Supreme Court." Other major points in his program were farm relief, labor legislation and unemployment relief, along with local improvement projects.

The young Texan stumped his 10th District with Johnson vigor and spoke in terms his friends and neighbors understood.

"It didn't take me long to decide on the main plank in

my platform—or the others," he told them. "I didn't have to hang back like a steer on the way to the dipping vat." He pointed out that, only a year before, Roosevelt had been elected to a second term by a majority of more than ten million votes and had carried forty-six of the forty-eight states.

"The trembling, fear and reaction of the estimable Eight in the Dark are only a ripple on the surface (of national public opinion)," he said. "They alone subscribe to their awful prophecies that destruction, carnage and utter ruin will follow if the government keeps pace with changing times.

"I'm for the President," he continued. "When he calls on me for help I'll be where I can give him a quick lift, not out in the woodshed practicing a quick way to duck."

The Johnson strategy proved good. He attacked the Eight in the Dark and they in turn centered all of their fire on him, lifting him into the spotlight of publicity and attention.

He told the voters that this election, far from being insignificant, was the focus of the nation's interest as a test of Roosevelt support in conservative Texas. He tied his campaign to Vice President John Garner and House Majority Leader Sam Rayburn, both Texans, and to "the most powerfully united delegation in Congress—the Texas delegation."

"It has," he said, "stood out like a rock when others have weakened in their faith or chased after strange or idiotic spooks."

Prophetically, he concluded:

"If the administration program were a temporary thing, the situation would be different. But it is not for a day or a year, but for an age. It must be worked out through time and long after President Roosevelt leaves the White House it will be developing, expanding."

The campaign was in many ways a family affair. Lyndon Johnson's mother usually sat on the platform at speakings. His wife was with him as he toured the ten counties of the 10th District. And many of the older boys and girls he had helped and hired during his NYA days—with their families —turned out to work enthusiastically for their former chief.

Two days before the election, Johnson went into an Austin hospital for what was announced as an emergency operation for appendicitis. One of the President's old Texas friends, who was working in the campaign, said recently:

"I'm not sure how much of an emergency it was. Seems to me Lyndon had been complaining about that appendix for some time. But this sure was a good time to have it out —at least as far as the publicity was concerned."

In any event, the candidate was still in a hospital bed when the reutrns came in, during the night of April 10, 1937. He had won, with almost twice as many votes as his nearest opponent. Since this was a "sudden death" election, with the leading candidate declared the winner, no runoff was necessary for a majority.

So, Lyndon Johnson returned to Washington, this time as the duly elected Representative of the 10th District, which encompassed both Johnson City and his birthplace near Stonewall. He was twenty-nine years old.

5

☆

Congressman Johnson

When the smoke of the election, and the fumes of the anesthetic from his appendectomy had cleared away, and when Lyndon Johnson found himself incontestably elected to Congress, he received a royal political command.

Franklin D. Roosevelt was cruising off the shores of Texas in the Presidential yacht at the time and he sent word to Governor James Allred that he would like to meet this young belligerent from the Texas Hill Country who had fought—and won—under the colors of the New Deal. Allred took Johnson to Galveston when the yacht docked there, and introduced him to the President, who was leaving ship for a special train. Roosevelt invited Johnson to ride across Texas with him, an invitation many Congressmen would have traded their seniority for. The young Congressman accepted, of course.

Back of President Roosevelt's wish to meet Johnson, and of the significant invitation which followed it, lay a story of the national political situation of the times.

In the election of 1936, Franklin Roosevelt had swept

forty-six of the then forty-eight states in the greatest American political victory of modern times. Some of the leaders
of his own party, after the moments of early jubilance,
found themselves viewing this overwhelming victory of the
man in the White House—for it was primarily his alone—
with disparate sentiments. The grandeur of the triumph
was easily translatable into power and it was the power of
one man, not of the party.

One of these doubters was John Nance Garner, Roosevelt's Vice President in both 1932 and 1936. The former
Speaker of the House, Garner had been called "a whisky-
drinking, poker-playing evil old man" * and the "Sage of
Uvalde," meaning Uvalde, Texas, his home town, depending on the point of view of the namer. Garner, with his
eye on the 1940 Presidential nomination, had a very personal interest in the setup. He probably had honest convictions in looking with some alarm on a Democratic party
situation where one man stood so far above the crowd he
obscured all others with his shadow. There were many who
shared this viewpoint.

It was into this atmosphere of unease that Roosevelt
tossed his plan to increase the membership of the Supreme
Court and it gave his dissident lieutenants a ready-made
issue. There was a certain sacredness to the image of the
Supreme Court, and equally, a certain sacrilege in "packing" its membership in order to liberalize its opinions on
New Deal legislation.

In the spring of 1937, the "Court packing" measure was
before Congress and it was evident from both popular and
legislative sentiment that it faced rough sledding in both

* By the United Mine Workers' John L. Lewis.

houses. The Texas delegation, almost certainly to some extent inspired by Vice President Garner, was solidly against the bill.

Thus, when Lyndon Johnson ran for Congress in the 1937 special election, word had gone down to the Lone Star State from the Texas Congressional leaders to discourage any campaign support for the Supreme Court measure. Everyone, you might say, got the word but Lyndon Johnson. Whether he ignored the message as a matter of principle, whether it was his admiration for Roosevelt and his New Deal theories, or whether he just wanted to win is not a matter of record. More than likely it was a combination of all three.

In any event, Johnson's campaign as a rampant New Dealer and his victory over some eight opponents who denied the Roosevelt cause, attracted the attention of the White House, and the President went out of his way to look up the young Texan and show approval. It was a signal political beginning for the man who is President today.

During much of the Roosevelt Administration, Thomas G. Corcoran was a New Deal "brain truster," an author of New Deal legislation and behind-the-scenes strategist. He worked out of the Reconstruction Finance Corporation, as special counsel, but his habitat and field of toil were centered in the White House. He was sometimes known as "The Invisible President." What was his job?

"I did everything," said Corcoran, now a successful Washington corporation lawyer. He has lost none of the ebullience and Irish charm, nor the bumptiousness which caused Franklin Roosevelt to name him "Tommy the Cork" some twenty-five and more years ago. In 1960 Corcoran supported Lyndon Johnson for President.

"The first time I ever heard Lyndon Johnson's name was in 1937," recalls Corcoran. "Aubrey Williams was head of the National Youth Administration.

"I ran into Aubrey at the White House and he said, 'For heaven's sake call a young man named Lyndon Johnson in Austin and tell him not to run for that house seat. He's my whole operation in Texas and he's a lot more valuable to NYA than he would be in Congress.' "

Corcoran tried to call Johnson, couldn't reach him immediately—and then it was too late. Johnson had announced his candidacy.

"Then," said Corcoran, "the Boss met Lyndon in Galveston and invited him to ride across the state in his train. That was all it took—one train ride." At the end of the trip, Roosevelt had found a protégé and Johnson a mentor. It would be hard to say who won whom. Corcoran continued:

"By the time Lyndon arrived in Washington the word had gone out: 'Be nice to this boy.' The Navy was the President's pet. He asked Carl Vinson to put Johnson on the Naval Affairs Committee (the powerful predecessor of the current House Armed Services Committee) and there he became Vinson's pet." (Representative Carl Vinson of Georgia was Committee Chairman.)

"Lyndon was an operator, but he operated for good causes. He got more projects and more money for his district than any other man in Congress—but they were worthwhile projects and they were good for the people."

As a favorite of President Roosevelt, Johnson made friends with the "inner circle" at the White House. He was personally close to Tommy the Cork and to James Roosevelt, the President's son. Grace Tully, the President's secretary liked him.

"He could always get to the President," said Corcoran, "and this information got around. He found other Congressmen were asking him for favors; his prestige on Capitol Hill was skyhigh."

Corcoran also remembers his first meeting with Lyndon Johnson. It was at the White House, soon after the newly-elected Congressman arrived from Texas. Under his arm he had photographs of the Buchanan Dam and plans for a project to supply rural electrification to the farmers and ranchers of his Hill Country 10th District.

The Buchanan Dam, named for Johnson's predecessor in office, is one of a series thrown across the Colorado River, a stream which is wholly contained in Texas, flowing six hundred miles from Dawson County to Metagorda Bay, on the Gulf of Mexico.

It had been built in the early 1930's as part of a state reclamation and flood control plan, with a parallel purpose of producing cheap electric power. Lyndon Johnson wanted this power carried to his district, an enterprise which would require federal funds. He had been told by bureau chiefs that his Hill Country was too sparsely populated and his idea uneconomic. Typically, he went to the fountainhead of authority.

"Lyndon didn't go to the President with just an idea," said Corcoran. "He had a big picture of the dam, and detailed figures on power requirements, costs and consumer usage."

Conscious of the fact that the President was both accustomed and inured to conversational bombardment, the young Texas Congressman spoke little. He showed his picture and explained his figures. He said the children of his constituents deserved to grow up in a better life than he had, and his father and grandfather had. Then he kept still and let the President talk, and when he walked out, he had Roosevelt's promise of approval.

Johnson's fight to get electrification was two-pronged and had to be waged on two fronts. The first, and the subject of his talk with Roosevelt, was to obtain approval of the necessary federal funds to bring the electricity to his district, where he would be available for local co-operative organizations. Secondly, he had to inspire the organization of the necessary co-ops.

Working with the recently established Rural Electrification Administration, he stumped his district, first for the formation of co-ops and then in the battle of public power against the privately owned "power trust," which had long furnished electricity to Texas with financing from New York. New Deal sentiment was, of course, strongly on the side of the co-ops and against "Wall Street." Johnson won his battle on both fronts. By organizing the biggest co-op in the nation, the Pedernales Electric Co-operative, with headquarters in Johnson City, he proved that his Hill Country constituents were as eager to have the convenience of electric power as their city cousins were. With the announcement of its approval, in September of 1938, he said:

"It isn't talk any more for farm women, to whom electricity has always been a faraway thing. Within a few months, they can lay aside their corrugated washboards and let their red hot cookstoves cool off while they iron on a hot August afternoon.

"The farmer who has been dragging water out of a well with a bucket all his life can not only get himself an electric pump to do the work, but he will have power he can afford to buy to run it."

Johnson's words were accurate. In his district, when the co-op was finally under operation, rates for electricity were twenty-five per cent cheaper than they had been in neighboring areas, and the co-operative movement caught on to spread throughout Texas.

His work culminated, in 1939, when the Lower Colorado River Authority purchased the plants and equipment of a complex of privately-owned electric companies in sixteen Texas counties, most of them in Johnson's 10th District.

It was during his fight to get electricity for his farm and ranch constituents that Johnson formed his association with the late Alvin Wirtz, counsel for the Colorado River Project. It was Wirtz, with his German levelheadedness, who more than anyone else tempered the Johnson enthusiasm and impetuosity with a steady, solid common sense and, above all, organization of effort.

"Lyndon had a number of good angels," said Tommy the Cork. "Roosevelt was one. I probably helped. But Alvin Wirtz was the best of the good angels."

These were the days when the government was pouring millions and millions of dollars into the economy to end the recession. The Reconstruction Finance Corporation and other government agencies were looking for worthwhile projects which would provide employment, aid the economy and produce a lasting benefit.

Johnson, with the help of Alvin Wirtz and Austin construction experts, made it easy for federal administrators to approve his undertakings. As he had gone to the President with the figures and facts of his first electric project, he also approached other enterprises with the same sure touch. He didn't just have an idea, a plea. He had plans, working drawings, cost estimates and projected estimates of the results.

"His causes were always solid," said Tommy the Cork. "They always helped people."

And they almost always had the touch of humanity. A half-million-dollar slum clearance proposal in Austin followed a walk through the city one night. To get it approved, he stirred up sentiment with speeches and radio addresses, describing scenes such as this:

"Last Christmas, when all over the world people were celebrating the birth of the Christ Child, I took a walk here in Austin, a short walk, just four blocks from Congress Avenue (the main downtown street). There I found people living in such squalor that Christmas Day was to them just one more day of filth and misery. I found forty families on one lot, using one water faucet, living in barren, one-room huts. There was no electricity.

"One typical family—living in one room without a single window—slept, cooked, ate there, while the mother bent over a leaky tub, washing clothes for the little money they had; the father lay ill with an infectious disease. There were ten children, all under sixteen."

These were Mexican-American or Negro, families and most Texans, at that time, could walk through the same scene without translating it into terms of personal degradation and suffering. It was part of the landscape, a pile of refuse in a weed-grown lot; they simply didn't see it. Johnson did, perhaps because there had been so much poverty in his own life, personal and observed.

When he discovered in these depression days that government agencies, set up for that purpose, were making small loans to white farmers to buy seed and equipment, but were not making the same loans to Negroes, he raised —in a Texas phrase—"unshirted hell." Many of the Negro farmers were just as good risks as the whites, he said, and some of them were better. Their applications began to be favorably processed almost immediately, and Washington officials were impressed that a Southern Congressman was taking time and trouble for the Negro.

During Lyndon Johnson's first two years as Congressman he obtained more than seventy million dollars for his Hill Country district in federal loans, grants and projects— electric power, slum clearance and other undertakings which were carried out by the Works Progress Administration and the Public Works Administration. It was something of a record for a freshman Congressman; a tribute to the careful planning which marked every enterprise, including those in which Alvin Wirtz frequently helped. Johnson, in turn, was more than helpful in securing for Wirtz the appointment of Under Secretary of the Interior in 1940. When Wirtz died in 1950, Johnson lost one of his greatest friends.

Johnson's stature in Congress rose steadily. He was a man who could get things done, a characteristic he has never lost. Sam Rayburn, who became Speaker of the House in 1940, was a good friend, as were other members of the Texas delegation. Johnson's voting inclinations were normally with the New Deal, but when New Deal measures conflicted with the Johnson beliefs (usually on some form of farm aid), he could and did vote with his conscience.

Politics in his own Hill Country district gave him little or no trouble; to his constituents he was their man in Congress. Because of Lyndon Johnson, they could push a button and get lights and heat and power. Government projects in the 10th District meant jobs, meat on the table and money in the till. He had the lighest of opposition for his first full term in 1938 and again in 1940.

Lyndon Johnson was a delegate to the Democratic National Convention in 1940, where he saw his fervid hopes realized in the nomination of Franklin Roosevelt for a third term as President. He also witnessed John Garner fail in his bid for the Vice Presidential nomination and his retirement from politics. Dropped by Roosevelt, he was replaced as running mate by Henry Wallace.

Typically, Johnson helped maneuver the Texas delegation to that convention away from a touchy conflict of interest. With Roosevelt's approval, he and Sam Rayburn worked out a plan with other Texas delegates whereby the Texas group would go to the convention committed to Garner—but only to the point where it became clear he had no chance for the nomination. Throughout it all, Johnson and Garner remained friends.

During this 1940 election campaign, Johnson performed yet another yeoman service for the Democratic Party and his great friend in the White House. Roosevelt was running against Republican nominee Wendell Willkie. While the odds were good that FDR would win, Willkie still had a great popular following and it was quite possible that Republican candidates for Congress, running under the Willkie banner, would pick up enough seats to gain control of the House.

Normally this would have been a matter left to the labors of the Democratic Campaign Committee, but neither House Speaker Rayburn, nor Floor Leader John W. McCormick of Massachusetts, had much faith in the Committee. Confronted with the problem, President Roosevelt asked for suggestions.

"Put Lyndon Johnson on the job," said Rayburn. Roosevelt did.

Moving into an unlisted office with a small staff and a battery of telephones, Johnson went to work. The primary need was for money to distribute with judicious care. Lyndon Johnson got it, mostly by tapping sources of wealth who were against Roosevelt—and wouldn't contribute to his campaign—but who did want to maintain a Democratic House of Representatives. It was coincidental that most of the sources of revenue were Texas millionaires who were even then realizing it was better to have Lyndon Johnson *for* you than otherwise. And the phone requests they got were personal appeals.

The Texas Congressman raised something over $60,000, which was disbursed for the care and voting welfare of some one hundred and fifty Democratic candidates. Instead of losing the House, the Democrats picked up six seats and no one forgot who did it, least of all the winners.

The third Roosevelt administration went into office with the almost certain realization that the nation could not much longer avoid being swept into World War II. These were the days of lend-lease and Bundles for Britain. Already American industry was gearing itself to a war footing. Newly-built plants were competing for workers—women as well as men. "Rosy the Riveter" pulled on slacks for her first job.

That Lyndon Johnson realized the inevitable entry of the United States into the war, and foresaw the need for defense is clearly apparent from his Congressional action of those days.

On March 21, 1938, he voted on the final passage of a bill to add additional vessels to the U.S. Navy.

On February 23, 1939, he voted against an amendment which would have blocked the fortification of Guam.

On May 8, 1939, he voted for final passage of a bill to still further increase the size of the Navy.

On June 22, 1939, his vote helped kill an amendment to cut appropriations for 1,283 new military aircraft and increases in Army funds.

On June 30, 1939, he voted against an amendment to prohibit the shipment of arms to the belligerent nations which later became our allies; later in the day, he voted on final passage of the Neutrality Revision Act (which had the effect of permitting us to aid, chiefly, Britain).

On September 7, 1940, he voted *Yes* on final passage of the Conscription Bill to set up a system of compulsory military training and service—the draft. (The war in Europe had been under way for one year.)

On March 19, 1941, he voted for supplemental appropriations to provide aid to the government of any country whose defense the President considered vital to the defense of the United States.

On August 12, 1941, he voted for a measure declaring a national emergency, extending terms of enlistments, appointments and commissions in the Army.

The war in Europe and defense preparedness activities in this country made Lyndon Johnson's position on the Naval Affairs Committee increasingly important and the 10th District Congressman found his sphere of influence widening to include all of Texas. He was instrumental in locating the huge Naval air training base at Corpus Christi, and the Naval Reserve Station near Dallas, also in establishing a Naval ROTC unit at the University of Texas and in placing ship building yards at Houston and Orange, Texas. None of these was in his district.

In April, 1941, on the death of Texas Senator Morris Sheppard, a special election was called to name a successor. The story of how Lyndon Johnson made his announcement for the Senate seat, from the White House door, is by now an historic incident.

He had called upon President Roosevelt and, after a brief conversation with FDR, emerged to tell reporters he would make the race. Later, in a press conference, the President was asked to comment.

"It is up to the people of Texas to elect the man they want as their senator," he observed. "Everyone knows that I cannot enter a primary election.

"To be truthful," he continued, "all I can say is that Lyndon Johnson is a very old, old friend of mine."

When the laughter had subsided, he authorized the newsmen to quote verbatim from his remarks and word went out that Johnson had the "blessing" of the White House.

The campaign was another of the multi-ringed circuses which Texas loves so well, complete with a dozen spangled performers, fun for all and a "sudden death" finish, that is, the candidate polling the most votes wins without a runoff.

In this campaign, everyone got into the act. The three center rings were occupied by Texas Congressman Lyndon Johnson, Texas Governor W. Lee ("Pass the Biscuits Pappy") O'Daniel and Texas Attorney General and All-American Quarterback, Gerald Mann. Another candidate, who didn't quite make the center spotlights, was Texas Congressman Martin Dies, Chairman of the Un-American

Activities Committee in the United States House of Representatives.

Others in the race for Senator, but never seriously considered by the voters except for their entertainment value, were Dr. John R. Brinkley, who peddled goat gland rejuvenating powders via a radio station across the Mexican border; two descendents of Texas-Mexican War heroes; an ex-bootlegger; a Baptist minister; one man who gave away mattresses to the families (in his audiences) with the most children; a chiropractor and half a dozen assorted others.

"Pappy" O'Daniel was another of those phenomena who appear on the Texas political scene with no visible reasons for support from voters other than bizarreness. "Pappy" had been a flour salesman and, in the course of selling, discovered the radio. He already had a guitar and a collection of hillbilly songs and he had parlayed these holdings, with the help of three attractive youngsters of his own, Pat, Mike and Molly, into the governorship. Now he was trying to repeat in the Senatorial race. He was a good entertainer; he was an "aginer" (of wicked vested interests); and he had a diabolical talent for turning an opponent's words against the speaker. When a newspaper account mentioned that his mother had done the family laundry, as most Texas mammas did in those days, he cried:

"You know what they're sayin' about me now? They're sayin' that my poor old mother was a washerwoman." The votes rolled in.

Martin Dies was violently anti-administration, while Gerald Mann stuck to the middle of the road and went after the younger people and the football vote. (Mann ran third.)

Johnson made a valiant effort to conduct a respectable

campaign—until it became obvious that his chief opponent was "Pappy" and to compete with the flour salesman you had to get somewhere near his level. So Lyndon added his own musical combo, a 275-pound singing star billed as the Kate Smith of the South and defense bond giveaways. He was the first Texas candidate to campaign by airplane. He sought votes on a platform of national peril, increased preparedness and support for the President. He had voted for the draft and he promised his audiences that, if their sons were sent to war, he would leave his seat in Congress to join them.

He lost the election by 1,311 votes out of a total of nearly six hundred thousand cast. He might have contested.

"No," he said. "That's the ball game. Let's go back to work."

When the Japanese bombed Pearl Harbor five months later, he was as good as his word. Along with other mother's sons, he went to war.

6

☆

Lieutenant Commander Johnson
in World War II

On May 21, 1942, a Navy Flying Boat, PB–2Y Coronado, by official designation, landed in the harbor of Noumea, on the island of New Caledonia, sending up a spray of clear water as it taxied toward shore and the beaching ramp. The muzzles of her fifty-calibre machine guns glinted dully in the hot sunlight.

The first man to leave the craft was Admiral Roberts C. Ghormley. He was on his way to Auckland, New Zealand, to establish a South Pacific Navy Headquarters.

The second man off was a six-foot-three Texan who had left his elected seat in the United States House of Representatives two days after Pearl Harbor to wear the uniform of a Naval Lieutenant Commander—his name, Lyndon B. Johnson.

May was not an auspicious month for America in the Pacific Area, during World War II. Corregidor had fallen on the fifth. The Japanese now held all of the Philippines.

Their fleet had been stopped at the Coral Sea, but the battle had taken a heavy toll of American aircraft and crews. New Caledonia itself was an island of tenuous safety.

The naval and air strength of the United States in the Pacific was desperately thin. It was scattered and threaded over the thousands of miles between the North American continent and Australia, fighting to contain an enemy whose long-laid war plans had included overwhelming superiority in every phase of operation.

Lieutenant Commander Johnson was on a special mission for the President of the United States, to inspect and assess the state of that fighting strength—its equipment, supplies, communications, men and morale—and to report back to Franklin D. Roosevelt personally with his findings.

In addition to being a member of the Naval Affairs Committee of the House of Representatives, Lyndon Johnson had been for several years a member of the Naval Reserve. On December 8, following the bombing of Pearl Harbor, the Congress declared war on Japan.

One hour after voting "yes" on the motion, Johnson requested the Navy to call him up for active duty. One day later, on December 9, he was in uniform, the first member of the House to enter any of the services in World War II. Mrs. Johnson held down his desk during his absence, handling all those things she could, sidetracking or postponing others, performing efficiently and effectively without pay. Lyndon Johnson himself had notified the House Sergeant-at-Arms to stop his salary as a representative and during his service in uniform the Johnsons received from the government only the pay of a Navy lieutenant commander.

Johnson's first appointment with the Navy was at San

Francisco, where he was assigned to the office of the Chief of the United States-New Zealand Command. The Navy did not for one moment forget that Johnson was a member of the House of Representatives, more, that he was a member of the Committee on Naval Affairs and—reef the top gallants, men—that he was a friend and protégé of President Roosevelt. The assignment in San Francisco had a ringing sound of importance, but it was safe. And it was pleasantly located.

Unwisely, the Navy had not taken a clear sighting on the Lyndon Johnson temperament. He hadn't gone to war to sit quietly in the back water and he hated shuffling papers. He broke away at the first available moment, flew to Washington and saw the President.

When he walked away from the White House he had an assignment which threw him into the midst of history's biggest combat zone, where, for several weeks, he learned about the war at first hand, including how it feels to be shot at.

Across the Potomac River from the White House, in the newly-built Pentagon, the War Department and the Army General Staff had recently felt a similar need for like information from the Pacific. Hundreds of ships, hundreds of aircraft, and thousands of men had been sent westward to places very few in the United States had known or cared about only months before. Communications both to and from these remote islands, harbors, airfields, and even continents were limited to the bare necessities—when they came through. Like the President, the Army wanted a first-hand report. The Navy certainly knew Commander Johnson was going. The Army may have been informed—or perhaps not.

Pictured at the ranch, the President, Luci Baines, Lynda Bird, and Mrs. Johnson

One of the first pictures ever made of Lyndon Johnson. He was six months old.

Lyndon Johnson as a boy, "in a pensive mood," his mother wrote in her scrapbook

The house where the President was born, just over the line in Gillespie County and about a mile from the present LBJ ranch

The LBJ ranchhouse with the communications tower in the background

The President and the First Lady at the entrance to the LBJ ranch

Lyndon Johnson, right, when a member of the college debating team

The fifth, sixth, and seventh grades at Cotulla with Lyndon Johnson, teacher, center

Lyndon Johnson with a group of NYA boys and girls in Texas

Campaigning in Texas for the Senate in 1941

The first recorded meeting of Lyndon Johnson and Franklin D. Roosevelt on May 12, 1937, at Galveston, Texas, after Johnson's first successful political campaign for Congress

Making a campaign speech from the porch of a Texas supporter's home

Lieutenant Commander Lyndon Johnson, 1942

Lyndon Johnson and his mother during a Texas Senatorial campaign

The Johnson family in 1948. The President holds Luci Baines.

Senator and Mrs. Lyndon Johnson on the Capitol steps in 1958

Lyndon Johnson with former President Eisenhower on the White House
steps in 1958

Lyndon Johnson with former President Truman, former Vice President
John Nance Garner, and Speaker of the House Sam Rayburn on a 1958
visit to Garner in Uvalde, Texas

The late President Kennedy, former President Truman, and the future
President Johnson

L.B.J. with Angel Macais, Mexican Little League champion in 1957

With his wife, and daughter, Lynda Bird, and two little girls, in Norway, September, 1963

The then Vice President Johnson with Mrs. Johnson on their trip to
India, where they made many friends

With Mayor Willy Brandt, walking near the East German border during
the August, 1961, crisis

The President riding herd on some cattle at the LBJ ranch

The historic swearing-in ceremony aboard U.S. Air Force One, on November 22, 1963, in Dallas. At Lyndon B. Johnson's right stands Mrs. Johnson and at his left Mrs. Jacqueline Kennedy. Administering the oath is Judge Sarah T. Hughes.

The Johnson family in a picture taken since Lyndon Johnson became President. Mrs. Johnson is at his left, Lynda Bird to his right. Luci Baines is in the rear.

The first that Samuel Anderson, Lieutenant Colonel, Army Air Corps, knew of this was when his immediate commander on the General Staff called him in late one afternoon and asked:

"Can you get away in a hurry to go to the Pacific on an inspection tour?"

"Yes, sir," replied Anderson. "I can be ready in a couple of hours." (He really thought he would leave in a week or so.)

"No need to hurry," said the general. "You don't leave until morning."

Similar notice was given Lieutenant Colonel Francis Stevens, U.S. Army, also serving on the General Staff. Anderson was to report on the air side of the war and Stevens on the ground fighting phase.

A series of further coincidences linked their trip with that of Johnson, and threw the three men together across thousands of miles and in and out of dozens of now-forgotten battle places. After one combat mission all three were decorated by General Douglas MacArthur, Stevens posthumously. He had not returned.

This was not a time for wasting either time or talent, so Lieutenant Colonel Anderson's orders included the chore of picking up a four-engine B–17 bomber at Hamilton Field, California, and delivering it to the 19th Bomb Group in Northeast Australia, a unit which writer William L. White made a legend in his book, *Queens Die Proudly.*

"I wasn't checked out in the B–17," recalls Anderson, "so I flew co-pilot. We had the normal crew and Stevens rode as a passenger.

"We got to New Caledonia about May 14 and immediately lost our airplane. The battle of Midway was coming up. Our B–17 was an "E" model, first of the Boeing Flying Fortresses to have a tail gun. It was also a bird in the hand as far as the local commander was concerned, and he way outranked me.

"So we sat on New Caledonia for a week—stranded. And then Admiral Ghormley came through. We met him and we met Lieutenant Commander Lyndon Johnson. We very quickly discovered that all three of us, Johnson, Stevens and I, were on identical missions and we decided to make our inspections together. Admiral Ghormley agreed to take us with him to Auckland, and to send us on in his PB–2Y to Australia." New Caledonia is one of the Loyalty Islands, lying off the east coast of Australia, between New Zealand and New Guinea.

Sam Anderson was promoted from lieutenant colonel to full colonel during the inspection trip, served throughout the war in both the Pacific and European Theaters of War and ended his career as a four-star Air Force General.

He retired in 1963 and lives in Washington, D. C. For a time, both during and after the war, Johnson and Anderson, and their families, saw each other frequently. The last meeting of the two men, as this is written, was during Johnson's tenure as vice president, when they sat side by side at the head table during one of Washington's innumerable banquet affairs at which Johnson was the principal speaker. He and Anderson reminisced pleasantly throughout the evening.

The dates, times, and places given here of the weeks following the meeting in New Caledonia are from the official flight records of General Anderson, which he very kindly requisitioned from long-dormant files for that purpose.

Many of the incidents and details of the adventure are from his remarkable memory.

Admiral Ghormley's flying boat, carrying the three inspecting officers, left New Caledonia on May 21 and flew to Auckland, New Zealand, where the admiral remained, sending Johnson, Anderson, and Stevens on to Sydney, Australia. They arrived on May 23.

The next day, they flew commercially from Sydney to Melbourne, at the southern tip of the continent, where General Douglas MacArthur had established headquarters as Commander-in-Chief, Southwest Pacific Theater, after his escape from the Philippines the preceding March.

The three men checked into the Menzies Hotel, where each had a single room. By this time, they were all on first or nickname basis—Sam, Steve and Johnny.

"We started calling Johnson 'Johnny,'" said General Anderson. "I've learned since that we are probably the only people who ever did. It just seemed natural at the time."

The next day, the trio reported to General MacArthur and were given a full treatment of briefings by officers from operations, intelligence, communications, and supply. The story of the war's progress in the Southwest Pacific Theater was topped off by a personal audience with MacArthur.

"It was pretty impressive," General Anderson declared. "Johnny, Steve and I sat at one end of the general's big office. He paced back and forth behind his desk. He would refer to a map occasionally, but he didn't need notes. He was giving us the big picture and he did a masterful job of painting. We were all a little awed by the man and certainly impressed."

The three young officers spent the next several days inspecting American and Australian supply, training, and cantonment installations in the Melbourne area. Anderson and Stevens reported to Lieutenant General George Brett, the senior air and army commander, while Johnson reported to his counterpart, Vice Admiral Herbert F. Leary.

It was not lost on General MacArthur and other ranking officers (as it had not been on the Navy) that Lyndon Johnson was the personal friend of Roosevelt, and that his report to the President, combined with the reports of Anderson and Stevens to General George C. Marshall and the Army General Staff, would be studied closely at the highest level in Washington.

"I would say," Anderson recalls, "that 'Johnny' got the VIP treatment. But that didn't influence his inspection. He's smart and bright. And very energetic. Steve and I had to move fast to keep up with him."

On June 3, the three inspecting officers took off northward, bound for Sydney, in General Brett's personal aircraft, "The Swoose," whose history was itself the history of the early war days of the 19th Bombardment Group.

"Swoose" was one of thirty-five Model "D" Flying Fortresses the 19th Group had picked up spanking new at the Boeing factory in Seattle before the war started.

When the Japanese bombed the Philippines after Pearl Harbor, the planes of the 19th were divided. Some ten or twelve were at Del Monte Field, on the Southern Island of Mindanao. The rest were at Clark Field, Manila. Those the Japanese bombers didn't get on the ground, the enemy fighters shot down through overwhelming numbers as the 19th went out in two's and three's to attack Japanese shipping.

"Swoose" was one of the few of those original thirty-five

that escaped. At this time, it had been converted to a transport—put out to pasture, someone said—as the newer model "E's" came along.

Painted on her side, along with the flak dents, bullet scars and nicks from the Australian desert sands, was a wryly debonair figure emblematic of her name, "The Swoose"—half swan, half goose. And beneath it, the incredulous query: "It Flies?"

As Johnson, Anderson and Stevens boarded "The Swoose" they learned they had an escort, inspired, it seems likely, by the high level calibre of their mission. Accompanying them were Brigadier General William Marquat of the Army ground forces and Major General Ralph Royce of the Air Corps.

The party spent one day in Sydney, where there were few military installations, and then continued on—June 4— to Brisbane. Here there were contingents of all three services, although the largest group by far were there to man the pens, tenders and other facilities for submarines. It was largely Johnson territory, but they all took the inspection tour.

On June 6, they flew in "The Swoose" from Brisbane to Townsville, on Australia's northeastern tip, where the 22nd Group and the remnants of the 19th Group were stationed. It was to the 19th, of course, that Anderson had started to deliver his bomber. Townsville was also an Australian seaplane base.

"The 19th was in bad shape by this time," General Anderson said. "They had been shot at from the Philippines to Australia and they were lucky to get any planes in the air. Everyone was hard put for supplies at that time. Lack of any kind of spare parts made maintenance a miracle.

Even getting stuff to repair sheet metal damage to the fuselage was a major problem."

Anderson had known the 22nd Group back at Langley Field, Virginia. They were equipped with two-engine Martin B–26 bombers. Lieutenant Colonel Dwight Divine, the Group Commander, was an old friend.

"I learned from Dwight," continued Anderson, "that a mission against the Jap air base at Lae—New Guinea—was scheduled for June ninth. I set it up with Divine to go along as an observer. Stevens and Johnson immediately requested to go also.

"I told them I thought their going was foolish. It was an air mission and I was an air officer. They weren't. Johnson was Navy. Stevens was Army."

Others tried also to dissuade the pair, Anderson remembers. Generals Marquat and Royce, conscious of a certain responsibility, particularly tried to talk Lyndon Johnson out of going.

"Johnny just shook his head," remembers Anderson. "He said he had come out here to observe the war and he wanted to observe it."

Early June 9, that 1942, the three inspecting officers took off with the 22nd Bomb Group, each riding in a separate B–26 Aircraft. The planes flew almost due north to Port Moresby and "Seven Mile Strip," the operational base seven miles from the port.

There the aircraft refueled and were armed with bombs. Their target, the Japanese air base at Lae (near Salamaua) was the operational airfield, as Anderson remembers, for the "Taiman Group" of Japanese bombers, called "Bettys" by the Americans. The "Bettys" bombed Port Moresby almost every day and night. There were, as well, enemy ground-based and Navy fighter aircraft at Lae.

Also assigned to the mission against Lae were three B–17s, the only aircraft the 19th Group could muster into the air that day, and twelve two-engine B–25 North American-made bombers from the 3rd Bomb Group, based at Charter's Towers, fifty miles southwest of Townsville. The B–17s and the B–25s, with longer range, were flying direct to the target from their Australian bases.

The battle plan called for the three units to go across the Stanley Owen Range in New Guinea and on into Lae about ten minutes apart.

The B–17s were to go first at high altitude, 18 to 22,000 feet. They were to drop their bombs, continue on for fifty miles and then turn right. It was hoped they would draw the defending Jap Zeros away from the target. It was a typical assignment for the 19th.

The B–25s were to follow in at very low altitude, drop their bombs and turn left. Following them would come the B–25s at medium altitude, 10,000 feet.

The mission did not go exactly as planned.

The B–17s went in at high altitude, dropped their "eggs," ran fifty miles on past and turned right as planned. But the Jap Zeros were not decoyed, at least most of them were not.

The B–25s went in at low altitude as planned and dropped their bombs. Then, through some miscalculation or garbled transmission of orders, they made a 180-degree turn and headed straight back over their entry path.

The Zeros followed right behind.

"We met the B–25s a few minutes from targets," said

Anderson, "and the Zeros immediately shifted all of their attention to us."

The B–26 normally carried a seven-man crew—pilot, co-pilot, navigator, bombardier, turret gunner, waist gunner and tail gunner. On this mission it is probable that the navigator was dropped because the navigation was so simple he was not required. In any event, Johnson, Anderson and Stevens were all riding in different planes as observers, positioned in the radio compartment just behind the pilot and co-pilot. By moving forward, they had good vision ahead and to the side. By climbing up a few steps, they could command 360-degree vision from the navigator's bubble over the radio compartment.

The armament on the B–26 consisted of seven fifty-calibre machine guns. From his spot aft, the tail gunner manned two. The waist gunner had two, also, one on each side of the fuselage slightly back of midship. There were two more in the top turret, handled by the bombardier. The seventh gun was in the nose, fired by the pilot or co-pilot.

Lyndon Johnson was flying in a B–26 piloted by Lieutenant Walter H. Greer (who survived the mission only to lose his life later in the war). Just as they were going into the target, and just at the time they met the defending Zeros, Johnson's plane developed trouble in one engine.

The engine didn't cut out entirely, but it lost power and, in a matter of seconds, fell behind the group headed for the target. In those seconds, the combat-wise Zero pilots saw that the B–26 was in trouble and singled it out for attack.

Lieutenant Greer jettisoned his bombs and dived. His aircraft could make about 210 miles an hour. The Zeros were nearly a hundred miles an hour faster.

Weaving and corkscrewing in violently evasive tactics that threw Johnson about the radio compartment, Greer sought the safety of a low-lying cloud. His crew had six guns turned to the rear, all of them blazing. The Zeros—six, maybe eight, the crew never remembered for certain—followed. One was hit and went down. The others came on, trying to match their gunfire with the maneuvers of the B–26. They hit the plane repeatedly.

It was a matter of minutes before Greer gained the sanctuary of the friendly cloud. He leveled off and took stock. The tail gunner was O.K., so was the man in the waist. The turret gunner reported the kill. Everyone was fine up front, Johnson included.

The pilot said, "We'll go on down," and headed the plane for the deck. There, fifty, twenty, even ten feet above the waves, still weaving and corkscrewing, he headed for home. The Zeros couldn't get under the plane and its formidable firepower was concentrated on the angle from which attack would come—the rear. There were a few enemy passes, then the B–26 was out of range and headed for home.

The aircraft limped back to Port Moresby. It was heavily damaged. The crew was badly shaken up, but, fortunately, there were no injuries. The crew, later, was credited with one Japanese Zero shot down. The future president had observed the war at very close quarters.

The other eleven B–26s went on to target and all made it back except the plane carrying Stevens. It apparently was shot down, although unobserved.

Anderson was flying with Lieutenant Walter Krell. Their plane had been badly hit by flak and Zero fire, including sufficient damage to the landing gear so that it would not

go down. Krell belly-landed the aircraft at Port Moresby
and Anderson and the crew walked away intact.

Johnson and Anderson spent the night in Port Moresby.
The American commander of the allied air forces there at
the time was Brigadier General Martin F. "Mike" Scanlon,
who had taken over the Governor's House as his headquarters and living quarters.

There were, he recalls, always visiting firemen from any
of the Allies and of sufficient rank to require special attention. There was no military mess and no club in the
normal military sense. The Governor's House was staffed
by the Patuan New Guinea natives and they were, Scanlon
remembers, "good cooks." The food served at Government
House was mostly tinned. Occasionally, a plane flying in
would bring fresh beef, which was divided all around—and
on even rarer occasions, a bottle of whiskey. There were no
women, servants or otherwise.

Government House had a spacious veranda on three
sides and it was stocked with cots where everyone slept,
guests, air staff and commander alike, protected by mos-
quito netting. The weather was hot.

Seven Mile Strip itself had been hacked out of the jungle
and was primitive. Crews landed there for bombs and fuel.
Those timed to remain overnight ran their planes off to the
sides for concealment and the men slept either in or under
their craft until Scanlon persuaded the Australian ground
troop commander to have his Patuan workers build grass
huts for these battle-bound transients.

All supplies came in by ship and when the almost daily
and nightly alerts came, the craft scattered out to sea. When
the Japanese couldn't find a more interesting target, they
bombed the air strip.

Johnson and Anderson spent the night of June 9 on the porch of Government House, a fact recorded in Scanlon's diary. The general recalls Johnson as "very affable and pleasant."

Johnson's own recollections of that night in Port Moresby include meeting a pilot from Austin, Texas. He quoted the young Texan as wanting two things:

"Get us a better pursuit plane as quickly as you can, and get me word whether my new baby is a boy or a girl."

Johnson already knew about the need for a better pursuit plane (the official term "pursuit" was changed to the designation "fighter" after the war) and hoped to do something about that. And a few weeks later, when he was in Austin, he moved in typically on the problem of the baby.

"I went to the wife's home," he said, "and there I found a baby girl eight weeks old. The wife had sent four cables to her husband but she knew they hadn't reached him for they hadn't been acknowledged."

"So I," said Johnson, "spent $18 I didn't have on a phone call to Washington. I asked the War Department to break its rules this once, and I am glad to be able to report that an official cable went out from the Pentagon to General MacArthur, reading, 'Please deliver this message to Lieutenant Wilson Ralston—baby daughter eight weeks old and wife doing fine.'"

"Mrs. Ralston got an acknowledgment a few days later that the message had been delivered."

The next day, June 10, Johnson and Anderson were picked up by "The Swoose," with Generals Royce and Marquat aboard, and all flew to Batchelor Field, Darwin. Darwin, at that time, was a seaport town of a few thousand people, sitting on the northeastern edge of Australia, near to nothing else civilized. It was, and is, a government-built naval base, with wide streets in anticipation of a population explosion which has not occurred. In those early war days it had one good hotel, a bandstand in the park for Saturday night concerts, and a zoo inhabited by kangaroos, emus, and koala bears.

Batchelor Field was forty miles away. It had been graded out of the brush in a country reminiscent of the sandier, more desolate parts of West Texas—as Johnson quickly recognized. Two air fighter groups were based there when the inspection team arrived.

On June 12, "The Swoose" and party took off on a catty-cornered flight to Melbourne, a route which bisected Australia from its northeastern tip to its southwestern point, and a flight of some 2500 statute miles. The crew of "The Swoose" at this time was about as experienced as a crew could be. As a unit, its members had flown combat over much of the far Pacific—Major Frank Kurtz, pilot, a former Olympic diver, holder of the Silver Star and Distinguished Flying Cross and (later) a lieutenant colonel at thirty-one; Captain Harry Schrieber, navigator; Master Sergeant Charlie Reeves, bombardier, and Master Sergeant "Red" Varner, a former West Coast embalmer, crew chief.

Aircraft crewmen this experienced shouldn't have gotten lost, but they did. When the estimated time had passed and they had not yet reached their checkpoint of Cloncurry, about a third of the way, Schrieber checked and found that his navigation instruments were malfunctioning. He informed the pilot that he "had no idea where they were." The radioman tried to raise contact, to get a bearing on their position, but could raise no one.

"I had been dozing," General Anderson relates, "and I

woke up to realize the pilot was flying in squares or boxes. It was pretty easy to surmise from this that we were lost. I went up and talked to the pilot and—we were."

The pilot kept flying his boxes, so many minutes north, the same number east, then south, then west, and so on, trying to find Cloncurry so they could land. The country was much like that around Darwin, rough, sparsely wooded and, above all, sparsely populated. It was then late afternoon, nearly dark, and the fuel was running low.

There was a choice at this time of either parachuting out and abandoning the plane, or of making a forced landing. Johnson voted with the others to stay with the plane and "ride it down."

Major Kurtz saw the light of a house and near it a field which looked clear. He "dragged" it twice, to see that it was clear of gullies and other obstructions, put his landing gear down and went in.

The landing was three-point, a little rough, but good, and the plane rolled along easily to high ground, where the wheels would not sink into the turf. It stopped and everyone got out.

The house with the light proved to be part of an Australian station, the equivalent of the American ranch, and within a few minutes the owner and ranch hands were swarming over the scene. Crew members and others present have described the reception and Lyndon Johnson's reaction. They coincide. This country looked like Texas and the rancher and his help looked like the voters Lyndon had been courting for years.

He went around to them all, introducing himself and shaking hands. He talked about ranching, about cattle and sheep, about prices and about tariffs on wool and hides. In a little while, he knew their first names and they knew his. He told Anderson these were "real folks—like Texans."

It was the consensus of everyone watching that he could carry that precinct if he ever wanted to come back and run for election.

The owner of the station took the grounded fliers to the house, where they had coffee, milk and cake while the owner called the nearest little town, Charis Creek. There he routed out the sheriff, who commandeered cars and hard-to-get fuel for them, and drove out to the station.

The crew remained with "The Swoose," but about midnight the others piled into the sheriff's cars and headed for the nearest sizable town, Winton.

"The first part of the trip was pure cross-country," continued Anderson. "There were no roads. I was riding with Johnny and it was rough going. The section was full of kangaroos. They didn't jump over and through the car—as someone else had related—but they sure ran alongside and out in front. Johnny thought it was a wonderful experience—we all did."

The party finally struck a road, Anderson recalls, and then a tavern. The sheriff roused the owner.

"We had some beer and whiskey and went on," said Anderson. "Johnny met everyone here, too."

They arrived in Winton about 7:00 A.M., on June 11, and went to a frame family hotel where they had breakfast and went to bed.

There was a military air strip and depot at Winton, from which fuel was dispatched out to "The Swoose." Refueled, the plane took off, flew to Winton, landed, picked up the passengers, and continued to Melbourne without incident. Anderson and Johnson remained there the next several days, both busily preparing the reports they would take back to Washington.

As the first officer from the Army General Staff on such an inspection tour, Anderson came in for considerable friendly attention. As an inspecting officer on a personal mission for FDR, and for his own natural gregariousness, Lyndon Johnson was probably the most popular military man in town.

"We had a hard time getting away," General Anderson said.

On their last day in Melbourne, June 18, when both men were packing to depart, they were summoned to General MacArthur's office. He told them he was awarding the Distinguished Service Cross posthumously to Francis Stevens, who had lost his life on the B–26 mission over Lae, and was awarding them each the Silver Star. Then he spoke directly to Lyndon Johnson.

"I still don't understand," he said, "why you went on the mission."

"General," replied Johnson, "a lot of these boys fighting out here are Texas boys. Some of them are from my district. I wanted to see what they're up against. And . . . I'm on a mission for the President of the United States, to learn all I can about this war in the Pacific and to take him back a personal report. I can't do that sitting in headquarters."

General MacArthur nodded understandingly. "We don't have any Silver Stars out here," he said, "and the citations haven't been written yet. But you can pick up the ribbons and start wearing them. The citations will catch up with you later."

They did. Lyndon Johnson's reads:

Under the provisions of Army Regulations 600-45, August 8, 1942, the Silver Star is awarded by the Commander-in-Chief, Southwest Pacific Area, to the following-named officer serving with the United States Army Forces in the Southwest Pacific Area:

LYNDON B. JOHNSON, Lieutenant Commander, United States Naval Reserve. For gallantry in action in the vicinity of Port Moresby and Salamaua, New Guinea, on June 9, 1942. While on a mission of obtaining information in the Southwest Pacific Area, Lieutenant Commander Johnson, in order to obtain personal knowledge of combat conditions, volunteered as an observer on a hazardous aerial combat mission over hostile positions in New Guinea. As our planes neared the target area, they were intercepted by eight hostile fighters. When, at this time the plane in which Lieutenant Commander Johnson was an observer developed mechanical trouble and was forced to turn back alone, presenting a favourable target to the enemy fighter, he evidenced marked coolness in spite of the hazard involved. His gallant action enabled him to obtain and return with valuable information. (AG 210.5/24)

By command of General MacARTHUR:

Addressing West Point cadets on his birthday, January 26, 1964, General MacArthur remarked on the President's trip to the Far East more than twenty years earlier, and of the B–26 mission.

"If I had known that this young officer was going to be President," he said, "I might have taken better care of him."

Johnson and Anderson flew commercially from Melbourne to Sydney on July 19, arriving after nightfall. The next day they were weathered in. On June 21, they left for New Caledonia by Navy PBY. When they reached there, Johnson was ill.

In shuttling back and forth across Australia and to New Zealand during the month of June, they had changed weather conditions almost daily. In Melbourne, it was winter. In Darwin and Townsville, it was summer. Brisbane and Sydney were in between. New Zealand was steaming hot. Johnson had come down with a severe cold.

The two men spent the night aboard a sub tender in the Noumea harbor, Johnson in the sick bay. The next day, despite the protests of the medics, Johnson joined Anderson aboard the PBY. Thirty minutes out he had a severe chill.

"All we could do for him," said Anderson, "was to put him in a bunk and wrap him in blankets." That day, June 22, they arrived in Suva, Fiji Islands (it was steaming hot, again), where Anderson put Johnson in the hospital. It was then under New Zealand operation, although the Americans took it over shortly afterward.

Johnson's illness was diagnosed as pneumonia and he remained there in the hospital for twelve days. Anderson remained a week, then flew on to Pearl Harbor, where he saw Admiral Chester Nimitz, the great Navy commander, who was later to get a fifth star as Admiral of the Fleet. Nimitz arranged that Johnson receive Naval supplies and medical attention.

Johnson reached home from his Pacific trip—twenty-eight pounds lighter, due to the illness—just after President Roosevelt issued his directive ordering all members of the House and Senate who were serving in the Armed Forces to return to their offices.

One of his last semiofficial duties as a Naval officer was to call upon Mrs. Stevens, to extend his regrets for the death of her husband at Lae, where he could easily have lost his own life.

Johnson's report to President Roosevelt when he returned to the United States was in the form of a four-hour breakfast conference with "the boss." The young officer stressed the need for more and better equipment. Example: "We have no plane which will match the Zero in the Pacific," he said.

He pointed out the need for better leadership and urged weeding out of service "the incompetent among our admirals, generals and others in high military position." He thought some of them were still depending upon the tactics of the Civil War, or at least the war of 1917-18.

He reported a bitterness among the fighting men at what they felt was "politics and business as usual" in too many places on the home front. In spite of this, he told newsmen as he emerged from the conference with President Roosevelt:

"There is one thing the Americans out there (in the Pacific) are not short of, and that is courage and guts and fighting spirit. They've got plenty of that."

When Lyndon Johnson resumed his seat in Congress in midsummer, 1942, he brought with him a firsthand knowledge of the war and the desperate need for equipment that would be put into the hands of the fighting men. He asked for and got the Chairmanship of a subcommittee of the Naval Affairs Committee for special investigations into Navy procurement methods and the top level management of its war effort.

He crusaded against waste wherever he found or suspected it—in over-staffed government offices, in procurement contracts, in military manpower and in war plant absenteeism. He broadened the scope of his subcommittee until its work commanded a larger staff than that of the parent committee.

He drafted the "Work or Fight" bill, which brought a bitter opposition from labor unions, among others, and which was passed in final form on February 1, 1945. It permitted the government to freeze essential workers in their jobs and to penalize those refusing war jobs.

"Today, when every plane, every tank, every rifle bullet counts, when the Nation is straining every nerve and sinew to supply these things to our armed forces in volume and in time, a most serious charge is being brought against American labor—a charge based on the high percentage of absenteeism now shown on the records of our war plants.

"I do not think that we can fling this blanket accusation against all American labor. I do not believe that we can lay the responsibility for the avoidable work failure upon the great body of loyal patriotic Americans who are giving to the farthest limit of their energies and skills to produce the tools of war. Nine out of ten of these workers are giving of the best that is in them.

"I do not think in fairness to them that we can allow the tenth—the loafer, the inexcusable absentee, the slacker—to hide his own identity among them and by that means shift the burden of blame for his own personal act of disloyalty to the whole body. It is up to us to devise a means of finding out who is who, name by name—and, once in possession of this knowledge, to disinfect our war plants of them— and our Selective Service has a very potent disinfectant for this type of vermin.

"Once this is accomplished, the great majority of our war

workers will be given the exoneration which they so thoroughly deserve. To those who have made this exoneration necessary, we say, 'The draft board will get you if you don't watch out.' "

The bill required defense contractors to furnish the War Manpower Commission with quarterly reports of absentees, and provided that lists of chronic laggards should be sent to draft boards.

In defending the measure, Johnson quoted figures of absenteeism in the aircraft industry—enough in 1942 alone, he said, to have built four thousand bombers. Investigations by his committee uncovered the fact that thousands of able-bodied Navy enlisted men were occupying desk jobs. With the correction of this situation, another came to light —Navy abuses in requesting draft deferments for civilian workers.

When the war ended, Johnson was named a member of a newly-created House Committee on Post War Military Policy and from this vantage point fought the nation's frantic rush to dismantle the great war production industry which had been built up, and sell it at junkyard prices.

He protested the almost hysterical speed to reduce the American military machine to the shadow of strength which brought about the Korean situation a few years later. He was named a member of the House Atomic Energy Committee.

The death in 1945 of Franklin Roosevelt, the man who had been a "second daddy" to him, was a tragic blow to the Texas Congressman. Some years later, in 1953, he read to the Senate a formal statement of personal eulogy.

"Today marks one of the great events of American history (read Senator Johnson). It was on March 4—just twenty years ago—that the late Franklin D. Roosevelt took the oath of office as the President of the United States.

"In these times, we tend to forget the bleak mood of the country at the time he took office. The United States was clutched tightly in the grip of a terrible depression. Millions were unemployed, and walked the streets in an aimless search for jobs that did not exist. Corporation profits were nonexistent, and the ledgers showed few entries that were not in red ink. On farm after farm, the knock-knock of the sheriff's hammer symbolized the wave of mortgage foreclosures.

"Few of us can forget the feeling of confidence that swept the Nation when President Franklin D. Roosevelt took over the reins. He trusted the people and the people trusted him. Together—acting as Americans in a common enterprise—we proceeded to pull ourselves out of the mire of economic despond.

"It has been two decades since that great day. America has gone far and has lived through some of the most important chapters of history. Together, we have risen to the highest standard of living in history—to the position of the mightiest of the free nations of the world.

"We are still close to the administration of our late President. Many of the acts of that administration were and still are controversial, as are all events of the recent past.

"But there can be no doubt of the position of Franklin Delano Roosevelt in the hearts of the American people. He will always be the man who appeared in our darkest hour of depression and voiced the true soul of these United States.

" 'The only thing we have to fear is fear itself—' he said on March 4, 1933. Those are the words of hope which carried us through the depression. Those are the words of hope which can carry us through the days ahead."

7

☆

Senator Johnson

"Lyndon Johnson," said Tommy the Cork, "is a product of Texas where they make politics.

"In New York people make money. In Texas they make politics.

"Other men in the White House have been politicians, but they also had outside interests. They liked music or art or history or golf or sailing. Winston Churchill once said that the darling of the gods is the man whose business and pleasures are the same.

"Lyndon Johnson is that man," continued Thomas Corcoran, one of Johnson's "good angels" of New Deal days. "His grandfather was in politics. His father was in politics. Lyndon was born a politician, a Texas politician, where the science is an art. Whenever you see him doing anything else, you may be sure he would rather be politicking."

In 1948, with a dozen years in the House behind him, the Congressman from Texas faced the decision as to whether or not he should run again for the Senate. He would be forty that year. He could stay in the House with little opposition in his own district. Or, he could quit politics and make a better living for his growing family; his two daughters were one and four years old.

He had about decided on the latter course when, in May of 1948, he went to Austin to discuss the matter with old friends and supporters, before making an announcement that he would not run. In *The Lyndon Johnson Story,* Booth Mooney, a long-time Johnson aide, quotes Johnson on what happened:

" 'I got down there,' Johnson related later, 'and called in a few of my close friends and told them what I planned to do. There wasn't much talk about it, no display of disappointment on their part. They seemed to accept the decision.

" 'Then about four o'clock in the afternoon, a group of young men came to see me. I had known some of them since the NYA days. They had helped me in my 1941 race for the Senate. Some of them were making good records of their own in public service.

" 'They told me I had been the cause of their taking an interest in public affairs and working for better government. They said that gave me a certain obligation toward them. They asked me, quietly and without any argument, to change my mind about the Senate race.' "

It is easy to imagine that Johnson was, maybe, just waiting for someone to talk him into it, and they had. He called a press conference that night and announced his candidacy.

The race would not be an easy one, and Johnson knew it. Pappy O'Daniel, who had defeated Johnson in 1941 and whose conduct in the Senate for some five years had not enchanted his Texas supporters, declined to run a few days after the Johnson announcement. Already in the race, however, was Coke Stevenson, the war-time Texas governor who had retired from that office the year before. Stevenson was a rancher, conservative, deliberate, quiet—and popular. He had made hundreds of friends during his governorship. Lyndon Johnson was known chiefly in his own district. Coke Stevenson was known throughout all of Texas.

In his opening speech at Wooldridge Park in Austin, on May 22, 1948, Johnson set forth three "signposts" for the future of America and on these based his campaign. They were 1) Preparedness, 2) Peace and 3) Progress.

We must, he said, retain a strong Air Force, Army and Navy. We must maintain our industrial machine, built up in the war production years. As Chairman of the House Naval Affairs Subcommittee on Special Investigations, he had recently fought and won a one-man battle on this; just two weeks before the government had recalled 114 war production plants (preventing them being dismantled or put to other use). The saving, to the taxpayers, (for new ones) Johnson said, was a billion and a quarter dollars.

In the cause of peace, he declared, we must strengthen the United Nations, keep trade channels open and turn our atomic knowledge to peaceful uses. We must tell the war makers they can go this far and no farther—as we told Russia in preventing the disappearance of Turkey and Greece behind the Iron Curtain. He supported the Marshall Plan and programs designed to tell the World more about the United States.

The third signpost he called the most important. He said of it:

"With preparedness, and peace, will come progress, the third signpost on our road to a new tomorrow. Progress is made by men who look forward instead of backward; men who are doers instead of sitters; men who are constructive instead of just calculating.

"Here are immediate goals for progress:

"One. For the farmer, support prices; blacktop roads; electrified homes; soil and water conservation.

"Two. For the teacher, a salary as big as her job.

"Three. Laws protecting the public from both selfish labor and selfish capital.

"Four. Cost of living adjustments in old age assistance.

"Five. For public health, more hospitals, doctors and nurses.

"Six. A federal policy leaving to the states those matters which are state functions, such as civil rights.

"I have heard it said that the county courthouse should not be moved to Washington.

"But, can we look to the county courthouse to support farm prices and finance soil conservation? Who is there in the courthouse who can give us loans for electrifying homes; who in the courthouse will combat inflation?"

And, possibly because Lyndon Johnson was Texan enough to know his Southern, conservative Texas, he made points which he would not make today. They are interesting, not so much because he made them in running as the underdog in a Senate election, but in light of his later treatment of the same political problems when, as Senate Minority and Majority Leader and then Vice President, he felt himself serving all of the states and not just Texas. Moreover, these changes were made after the passage of ten years.

"The (present) civil rights program," he said in 1948, "is a farce and a sham—an effort to set up a police state in the guise of liberty. I am opposed to that program.

"I voted against the so-called poll tax repeal bill," he said then. "The poll tax (laws) should be repealed by those states which enacted them.

"I have voted against (appropriations for) the Fair Employment Practices Commission," Candidate Johnson said. "If a man can tell you whom you must hire, he can tell you whom you can't hire."

(As Senate Majority Leader and aiding the program of a Republican President, Lyndon Johnson shepherded through the Senate, in 1957 and 1960, the only two Civil Rights bills to be passed since the Civil War Reconstruction days. He made passage of still a third Civil Rights measure one of his major points with the 1963-64 Congress, after assuming the Presidency.

(He maintained his position on the poll tax, but helped pass the law which enabled the individual states to vote on a Constitutional Amendment abolishing the tax in federal elections. South Dakota, the 38th state required for a three-fourths majority of all fifty, passed the Amendment early in 1964.

(As Vice President, Johnson was Chairman of the President's Committee on Equal Employment Opportunities, a greatly advanced version of the FEPC. There, he was vigorously successful in fighting job discrimination.)

In trying to cover the 254 Texas counties, literally from Anderson to Zavala, Johnson found the motorcar and the train too slow. In a moment of inspiration, he turned to the helicopter; it was fast, easy to park and, equally important, attracted crowds. A great many people in Texas in 1948 had never seen a helicopter.

In mid-June, following a strenuous day, he broadcast over an East Texas radio station, saying:

"Good evening, ladies and gentlemen. This is Lyndon Johnson of Johnson City, Texas, the candidate for junior senator who is campaigning in East Texas from a helicopter that we call the Johnson City Flying Windmill.

"We'll broadcast from Huntsville at 8 P.M. over a station-wide network tomorrow night. I hope as many people as possible come out for these stops. We had fourteen hundred people today in Athens and big crowds all the way down to Lufkin.

"This campaigning by helicopter was a happy thought because the voters like to see a man before they vote for him . . . they like to shake his hand and look him in the eye and size him up.

"You people who listen to me over the radio want to know something about the fellow who is asking for your votes: what a candidate's background is, what he's done, what he believes in and what he will do with your vote. So that's what I'd like to talk with you about tonight.

"About my background . . . you might say that Lyndon Johnson is a cross between a Baptist preacher and a cowboy. Both of my grandfathers were veterans of the Confederacy—Sam Johnson founded Johnson City, and Joe Baines was a Baptist preacher."

The helicopter helped, but the campaign lacked fireworks and Lyndon Johnson knew it. He needed one good exciting issue, or one that he could make exciting—like the Court Packing issue which had sent him to the House in 1937. He couldn't get a rise out of his opponent; Stevenson was publicly ignoring him.

Then, late in June, state officials of the American Federation of Labor endorsed Johnson's opponent, an event without precedent in fifty years. Equally odd was the fact that Stevenson was far more the rich man's darling than labor's handmaiden.

The year before, 1947, the Taft-Hartley Act had been passed (over Truman's veto). It was a measure limiting union political activities and union powers. Labor bitterly opposed it. Lyndon Johnson had voted for it. Now, the labor endorsement gave him the red hot issue he needed. He opened the battle over Radio Station KNET on the night of June 23.

"Reports reached me today (he said) that a few labor leaders, who do not soil their own clothes with the sweat of honest toil, have met in a smoke-filled hotel room in Fort Worth and have attempted to deliver the votes of free Texas workingmen through the endorsement of a candidate without a platform, and a candidate without the courage to take a stand on the issues now confronting American labor.

"If there is an understanding between the labor leaders and their candidate by which he has agreed to vote for the repeal of the Taft-Hartley Act, then the rank and file of the voters should know it.

"I have called on this candidate repeatedly to say whether he favors or opposes the Taft-Hartley Act; how he would have voted on it if he had been in Congress; and whether he would vote for its repeal if elected to Congress.

"He has dodged these questions. He has told the voters that he will make them no promises."

The fact that probably half his rural audiences didn't know—or care—what the Taft-Hartley Act legislated made little difference. Johnson hammered at his theme throughout the campaign.

Stevenson led in the first primary with 477,077 votes to

Johnson's 405,617. Nine other candidates received a total of some 300,000 votes. Since no candidate received a majority, a runoff was necessary.

In the runoff, Johnson continued to plague his opponent with the dubious favor the state labor leaders had bestowed on him. He stressed his own war record, his stewardship of the 10th District as a Congressman, his friendship for the farmer and his eleven years' experience. He told his audiences a story:

"When I was a boy, my dad brought home to our rocky little cotton farm one day a brand new hired hand. This fellow admitted he hadn't ever chopped cotton, but he was willing to try. Dad took him out to the cotton patch, handed him a hoe, and pointed out the cotton and the cockleburs. When dad came back in about an hour, that man had the prettiest stand of cockleburs you ever saw, and there wasn't a stalk of cotton in sight.

"A man's willingness to do a job doesn't mean he can tell the difference between cotton and cockleburs. That's why I say experience in Washington is so important. I've been in training for this job as senator for eleven years. I've served an eleven-year apprenticeship in the House of Representatives."

It was a close runoff, even for Texas, with Lyndon Johnson the winner by just eighty-seven votes—polling 494,191 to Stevenson's 494,104. Certified as the Democratic candidate after several court battles, Johnson beat his Republican candidate in the general election two-to-one without campaigning.

Back in Washington, this time on the Senate side of the Capitol, Johnson settled down to political industry that changed only in detail and scope from his life in the House of Representatives. He was a junior Senator, but his constituency was all of Texas—and seven and a half million Texans. He didn't forget that, for all practical purposes, half of them had voted against sending him to the Senate, and this was a situation he must rectify. He enlarged his staff. Every letter was answered, promptly. Every visitor was seen and his problem—there was always a problem—attended. The phone wasn't permitted to ring more than twice. Johnson devised a box score to compile a record of callers received, letters written and phone calls made on behalf of constituents—for future campaign use. News letters and canned radio programs went back home regularly. When office funds were spent and the work piled up, Johnson hired extra help and paid for this from his own pocket.

In the transfer of interests and activities from the House to the Senate, the change was largely in scope. He had been on the House Armed Services Committee (formerly Naval Affairs). His old friend, Chairman Carl Vinson of Georgia, recommended Johnson to *his* old friend, Senator Richard B. Russell of Georgia, Chairman of the Senate Armed Services Committee, and Johnson was named a member of that group, a position for which he was eminently qualified.

When the Cold War started is a matter of some latitude for most of us. For Lyndon Johnson the Cold War started the day the Hot War stopped. Watching Soviet Russia swallow Poland, Czechoslovakia, the Latvian nations, Hungary and East Germany, he had fought the frantic dismantling of the great American war machine. Election to the Senate simply meant moving the field of battle. He became that body's conscience on preparedness.

When President Truman and his Defense Secretary Louis

A. Johnson (no relation) moved to cut the military budget well below even a reasonable danger point, Lyndon Johnson joined Senator Stuart Symington, first Secretary of the Air Force, in a continuing fight to prevent this. They battled for a seventy-five group Air Force and a comparable strength for the Army and Navy. They lost. When Congress appropriated defense funds over and above budget requests, these funds were impounded. Congress can appropriate; it cannot force the Executive Branch to spend.

With the signing of the North Atlantic Treaty, in March, 1948, Johnson used the opportunity to tell those who might oppose preparedness:

"How short is our memory. How soon we forget. To make us less forgetful, somewhere there should be a tablet of enduring bronze and on it inscribed two columns of names in everlasting letters.

"Above one column would read the inscription: Here are the names of those who refused to prepare. Here are the names of those who voted to send our Army home. Here are the names of those who thought our European friends beggars and tramps. Here are the names of those who voted against selective service, against the Marshall Plan, and said Communists wrote it, and against universal military service. That would be the heading on the first column.

"And on the other side would be eight short words: here are the names of those who died."

In February of 1950, the Senator warned:

"For five years we Americans have to some extent isolated ourselves behind the security of an atomic monopoly. We were tired from the exertion of war, weary of crisis. We have concentrated our national energy and our national talent on our own comfort more than on our security."

There was a wry justification of his words four months later, when South Korea was invaded. One month thereafter, Senator Johnson laid before his colleagues a resolution proposing the formation of a Preparedness Subcommittee of the Senate Armed Services Committee. The resolution was adopted and Lyndon Johnson was named Chairman. He selected his committee members with non-partisan care, choosing good talent from each side of the Senate Chamber. Members were: Republicans Styles Bridges of New Hampshire, Leverett Saltonstall of Massachusetts and unpredictable Wayne Morse of Oregon, at that time a Republican. Democrats were Estes Kefauver of Tennessee, Virgil Chapman and Lester Hunt of Wyoming.

Of the Subcommittee and its formation, Columnist Doris Fleeson wrote in the *Washington Star:*

"Congressional policing of the new war effort begins this week with the appearance of Defense Secretary Johnson before the Senate Armed Services Investigating Subcommittee whose chairman is Senator Lyndon B. Johnson, of Texas.

"Because an obscure Senator named Harry Truman parlayed an innocuous resolution for similar policing of World War II into the Presidency of the United States, unusual interest attach both to the subcommittee's plans and to the personality of its chairman,

"It is already being said that Lyndon Johnson wants to be President, which is legal. It can be added that ever since he entered the House in 1938 his bright brown eyes have been fixed on America's defenses from a front-row seat.

"This was the doing of his special patrons, Speaker Ray-

burn and Franklin Roosevelt, who persuaded shrewd Carl
Vinson that they had just the man for Mr. Vinson's select
Naval Affairs Committee. Thus the astonished House on
the Senator's first day in Congress saw him popped on the
powerful Vinson committee without that usual boring
interlude on printing or disposition of executive papers.
He has never looked back. A freshman Senator by grace of
eighty-seven Texas votes (his majority was eighty-seven),
he is on both the Armed Services and Interstate and Foreign Commerce Committees now.

"Obviously in a strategic spot, Senate Armed Services is
strongly manned; and it very quickly moved into the Korean crisis with a formal demand for explanations. This
demand was seized on by the quick-witted Mr. Johnson as
the band wagon for a new Truman committee. Within
twenty-four hours his resolution for a 'watchdog group'
was before his colleagues, who naturally were not averse to
so interesting and historically fateful a task."

At the first meeting of the Subcommittee, on July 31,
1950, Chairman Johnson told its members:

"Our assigned task is clearly defined in the resolution
adopted unanimously by the full committee. We are asked
to exercise both a continuous watchfulness and a continuous study of all policies, programs, activities, operations,
facilities, requirements, and practices of the Department of
Defense, the Armed Services, and other agencies dealing
with the national security in general and our present preparedness effort in particular.

"We are specifically directed to determine whether such
policies and practices are 'the most effective possible' and
to determine whether the administration of such policies
is 'characterized by maximum efficiency.' "

The Chairman also suggested certain "guideposts" of conduct, which he felt the members should keep in mind. He said:

"I. We will not hunt headlines. We will handicap—not help—our chances for success if we exploit the sensational rather than develop the substantial. It is my thought that the committee's work will be conducted primarily in executive sessions. Our reports will be reports to the full committee; we will not report directly to the Senate or the public.

"II. It is my sincere hope that politics can be left at the committee-room door. Our full committee has maintained a fine record of nonpartisanship. I hope we can emphasize unanimity so that here, at least, the Senate and public can expect to find uncolored, unemotional facts.

"III. Most important, I think this subcommittee must be extremely diligent not to establish—or attempt to establish—itself as a Monday morning quarterback club, second-guessing battlefront strategy. We were not created to tell the generals and admirals how to fight the battles, but rather to make sure that they and the men fighting under them have what they need to win those battles. Battlefront strategy is not a part of our duties and so long as I am chairman we will not get into that question."

The Korean War exposed in its first few weeks that the military economy of the previous two years had done more than cut the fat from the Army and the Air Force. American pilots fought Russian Mig jet fighters with World War II propeller-driven planes. At best, they had early model American jets which were far inferior. The Army wasn't equipped, either, to fight an almost guerilla-type warfare on Pork Chop Ridge and the other battlegrounds of mountainous Korea.

The war also revealed that something was radically wrong with our stock-piling program and our plans for emergency industrial mobilization.

The Subcommittee's first target was the Munitions Board, which was commissioned to pass on all sales of property in the national industrial reserve, that is, plants and facilities essential to military preparedness.

The subcommittee reported it had found that "the vast organization dealing with surplus disposal, rubber production and other matters made critical by the Korean War was proceeding at certain points on the continuing basis of the postwar policy of general demobilization."

Various surplus plants were being offered for sale at the very time that their productive capacity was needed for the war effort. Other surplus for sale included unused—but needed—motors.

"Since the Korean attack," Johnson said, "at least five properties in the reserve have been sold or have been in the process of sale, one of them without even a national security clause (which would enable the government to reclaim it)."

The report, which also criticized the Munitions Board's lack of cooperation with the Subcommittee, brought the prompt resignation of its Chairman, Hubert B. Howard.

The Subcommittee's vigorous investigation of Defense Department policies and sometime mismanagement brought also, on September 19, 1950, the resignation of Defense Secretary Louis Johnson, now remembered, among the military, as the first casualty of the Korean War. He was replaced by General of the Army George C. Marshall, wartime Chief of Staff, former Secretary of State and author of the Marshall Plan.

In 1952, Lyndon Johnson found himself part of the puzzling picture which made up Texas politics that year. Both the Democratic nominee for governor, and the junior Senator (Johnson was now Senior, replacing Tom Connally), announced for Eisenhower. Johnson, however, with Speaker Sam Rayburn, supported and worked hard for the Democratic nominee, Adlai Stevenson. Both also disagreed publicly with certain of his views—particularly on federal claims to ownership of oil-bearing Texas tidelands. Introducing the candidate in Austin, Johnson told his audience:

"It has been said that the Democratic Party could be improved. I will go further than that. I will say I have never seen the Democratic Party when it couldn't be improved. But I have never seen the Democratic Party when it wasn't an improvement over anything else that was offered.

"Ladies and gentlemen—here is the greatest improvement that could be offered by any party to the voting public. It is with pride as an American, Texan and a Democrat that I introduce the Democratic nominee for President of the United States—Governor Adlai Stevenson."

When General Eisenhower swept Texas, along with a good share of the nation, Senator Johnson took it calmly. He returned to his Senate seat in Washington, where he accepted the greatest political gamble of his life.

Senate Democratic Leader Ernest McFarland had lost his battle for re-election in Arizona to a conservative Republican, Barry Goldwater. With the Democrats now in the minority, this meant naming a Minority Leader. The Senators nominally in line for the post (by seniority) all declined because it was too politically dangerous. The Minority (or Majority) Leader is several things: he must formulate policy and carry it through; he must consider problems of the United States, not just his own state; he risks having his own constituents feel he is neglecting them; he is prominently in the limelight, particularly if he is not effective. Many senators are not interested.

Lyndon Johnson, with an eighty-seven vote majority in his only successful race for the Senate, at the youngest age in history, forty-four, took the job. The vote was unanimous, which meant mostly that forty-seven other Senators were relieved to see the position filled with a man they knew was competent. Neither the conservatives nor the liberals were exactly sure which should claim him as one of their own.

Actually, it was a job made to order for the restless, driving energy of Lyndon Johnson; for his talent of persuasion and his tremendous gift of finding a common meeting ground for dissident points of view. The year before, he had been named Majority Whip, a position in which his chief function was to round up his fellow Democratic Senators and get them on the floor when they were needed for critical votes. In it he performed well and he liked it. As Whip, he was also automatically a member of the Democratic Steering Committee and the Democratic Policy Committee. As Minority Leader, he was Chairman of both.

The Steering Committee makes assignments of Senators to the various regular committees. The Policy Committee makes decisions on the desirability, the importance and the priority of legislative programs in the Senate.

The new Minority Leader decided early on a program of action. Senate Democrats would oppose when it was a matter of policy to oppose. They would not oppose simply because they were the opposition party, and the man in the White House was a Republican. Johnson's views on the matter were succinct. He set them forth in a few words at a Jefferson-Jackson Day dinner in New York.

"There are two courses open to a minority party," he said. "It can indulge in the politics of partisanship, or it can remain true to the politics of responsibility. The first course is tempting to the weak, but ultimately it would be rejected by the American people. The second course is difficult, but is the road upon which we can offer leadership to the American people that will be accepted."

Johnson consolidated his position and improved the efficiency of the Senate by spreading the good committee assignments around, instead of adhering strictly to seniority. He saw that each freshman Senator had at least one important committee seat—on a committee in which he was interested—even when this meant cutting down some of the influence of his older colleagues.

The Minority Leader deftly used the famous Johnson tact and persuasion. Senators who thought their opinions were poles apart, suddenly found themselves in agreement, usually with the Johnson viewpoint. Frequently they wondered how it had happened! He coined the phrase of "saving Eisenhower from the Republicans" and helped the administration pass such measures—which he and the Policy Committee agreed were good for the nation—as the Mutual Security Bill, the Reciprocal Trade Agreement Act and other legislation to maintain defensive strength of the nation. When he felt legislation was not desirable, Johnson could be equally effective in turning thumbs down.

The year 1954 saw Lyndon Johnson elected to the Senate

for a second term by a margin of three to one. In this election, the Democrats also had a majority. Johnson, at forty-six, was now Majority Leader.

His desk for the next five years was the focal point of the Chamber. Of the job he did, James Reston wrote in the *New York Times* "Johnson is the best quarterback to come out of Texas since slingin' Sammy Baugh."

On the floor of the Senate, he was the manager and co-ordinator. In the cloak rooms and behind the scenes, he maneuvered, persuaded and compromised when he had to, saying: "American democracy was born in compromise."

He worked well with the Republican floor leaders, Senator Robert Taft, while he was alive, and, later, Senator William Knowland. Johnson became, many said, the second most powerful man in government.

He had a tremendous respect for the Senate and strong convictions as to the moral probity of men elected to that body. He could be tolerant, but when Senator Joseph McCarthy (probing alleged Communists in government) climaxed a series of offenses by referring to the Senate Select Committee members investigating him, as "handmaidens of Communism," Johnson could have no more of McCarthyism. On the Senate floor he said:

"On the basis of the evidence, it is my intention to vote for the (McCarthy) censure resolution. That is a personal decision on my part. I am not seeking to influence anyone else.

"I have searched my conscience carefully and can come to no other decision.

"In my mind, there is only one issue here—morality and conduct. Each of us must decide whether we approve or disapprove of certain actions as a standard for Senatorial integrity. I have made my decision.

"In making the selection, we sought men of prudence, men with judicial temperaments, men of unquestionable patriotism, men who could succeed in putting their country ahead of any political or partisan consideration. It is my belief that we succeeded beyond the fondest expectations of the most optimistic.

"Many people are strongly in favor of the Junior Senator from Wisconsin; many are strongly opposed to him. I doubt whether any action we take here will meet with the full approval of either group.

"But the overwhelming majority of the American people are far more concerned with the integrity of the Senate. The integrity can best be preserved by a straight-out vote on the sole issue—morality and conduct.

"For myself—and I am speaking for no other person—I have made my decision."

In July of 1955, Lyndon Johnson suffered a heart attack which he later described as "about as bad as you can have and live." The attack came during the Fourth of July weekend. When the Senate convened on Tuesday, July 5, the Chaplain offered a prayer for Johnson. Then Acting Majority Leader Earle C. Clements read the first official bulletin prepared by the attending physician. It said:

"Senator Lyndon B. Johnson has had a myocardial infarction of a moderately severe character. He was quite critically ill immediately following the attack but his recovery has been satisfactory.

"His physicians agree that under no circumstances can

he return to his duties during this session. He cannot undertake any business whatsoever for a period of months.

"However, if there are no further attacks of a severe character and his recovery continues to be satisfactory, he should be able to return to the Senate in January."

At the suggestion of Senator Herbert Lehman (whose funeral Johnson was to attend after becoming President), the Senate stood for a brief silent prayer. Then a dozen Senators, from both sides of the aisle, one after the other, arose to pay tribute to the Senator from Texas. They praised his dedication to his country and his leadership and they wished him speedy recovery.

In the Bethesda Naval Hospital, Lyndon Johnson set about organizing his recovery as he had always organized other things in his life. For the first several days he was permitted to do nothing. Mrs. Johnson moved into a room next door and remained there for the five weeks her husband was in the hospital.

Then, as he began to get better, he was permitted small activities. He could read the daily papers and the Congressional Record (which he had read and digested daily for eighteen years). A few visitors were allowed, and then one of the girls from the office, to bring personal mail. Soon thereafter, a second suite, just down the hall, became the Lyndon Johnson office, manned by one, sometimes two secretaries. A battery of telephones was installed. Calls and visitors were received there. But it was all carefully gauged activity.

Although six feet three, the Senator's weight of 215 pounds was too much. He went on a diet. He had always been a chain smoker. On the way to the hospital in an ambulance, he had asked for a cigarette. The doctor shook his head.

"You may not be seeing much of cigarettes," he said. Johnson has not touched tobacco since.

As his recovery progressed, so did the stream of visitors to his bedside. They included President Eisenhower, Vice President Nixon, Adlai Stevenson, practically every Senator on Capitol Hill, Cabinet members and many old friends from the House. Was he doing too much, a friend asked?

"No," replied Johnson. "The reporters write of the visitors. They don't mention the nap I take every afternoon, or the quiet evenings with Lady Bird and the girls."

When he was permitted to leave the hospital, he took his family to the Ranch at Johnson City, where he spent most of the intervening time until January of 1956, when the next term of Congress began. That fall, Lyndon Johnson's name was placed in nomination for the Presidency, but it is doubtful that he took the move seriously. Stevenson was nominated on the first ballot.

During the next three years Johnson grew in national stature. His prowess and legislative accomplishments on the Hill became almost legendary. He had recovered completely from the heart attack.

Three of the most controversial bills of his Congressional tenure came up during this time, two of them Civil Rights and the third Federal Aid to Education. Of his conduct in engineering both Civil Rights measures through the Senate, James Reston of the *New York Times* wrote:

"Johnson is a Southerner, but not a sectionalist. More than any other man in public life, more than any other politician since the Civil War, he has, on the race problem, been the most effective mediator between the North and the South.

"He is the man who induced the Senate to accept the Civil Rights legislation which strikes at the disfranchisement of Southern Negroes."

Education has always been close to the heart of Lyndon Johnson, perhaps because he came so nearly being a "dropout" himself after his high school days in Texas. It was reflected in his work with the NYA, and the help he gave his law classmates at Georgetown University back in the early 1930s. His speeches today reflect his concern that they carry certain marks of erudition. He told his fellow Senators:

"There is no security except in people. The Atlas, the Thor and the Jupiter will be obsolete within a few years. And once they are obsolete there will be nothing left of our investment in them except the experience we have gained.

"But there is one investment in which the United States can never lose. It is the investment in the minds of our young people.

"Security consists of people who are alert, people who are vigilant, and people who are trained to cope with the tremendous problems of the modern world.

"We cannot cope with those problems unless we have men skilled in physics, chemistry, mathematics, astronomy, and all of the natural sciences, but neither can we cope with them if our training is solely in the natural sciences.

"We look for citizens who are broadgauged, who understand the workings of our system, who are conscious of the great heritage of our culture. We need men and women who understand Aristotle as well as Darwin; who are as

familiar with Shakespeare as they are with Einstein and
Newton. The time may come when we will have to take up
arms once again to defend our heritage. But we must know
what it is that we are defending, and even more important,
we must know the kind of world which we wish to extend
and create so that our descendants can live in peace and
progress."

When the Russians launched their first Sputnik in October of 1957, Johnson found it natural to include space and
its exploration within the scope of his interest in national
defense. He organized and became the first Chairman of
the Senate Committee on Aeronautical and Space Sciences.
It was this committee which wrote the National Space Act,
establishing NASA and the National Aeronautics and Space
Council, of which he became chairman, as Vice President.

The Act decrees that our exploration of space shall be
for peaceful purposes and Johnson was conscious of this
when he addressed the Senate in May of 1960, after the
successful launching of the first Midas spacecraft, a satellite designed to detect and deliver warning of an enemy
missile launching, as follows:

"In light of the current world situation, the successful effort to launch an experimental Midas satellite by the
Air Force could easily be one of the most significant events
of the year. It could easily outmode a great deal of current
thinking, and could make academic many of the disputes
which now divide the world.

"Behind the Midas satellite, there is the reconnaissance
satellite (Samos). This instrument—still in the future—can
give us accurate information as to what is happening on
the face of the globe.

"It seems to me, however, that we must look upon these

developments as more than merely weapons added to the military arsenal of the United States. If our vision is limited to methods of destruction, we shall not obtain the only truly worthwhile goal—a world of peace and a world of freedom.

"We live in a country which can flourish best in a world where secrecy and suspicion have been abolished. We have a system that can stand up under the closest scrutiny of other people seeking to find flaws in our way of life.

"For this reason, it would seem to me, as I have suggested before, that it would be wise for our country to launch a crash program to develop the reconnaissance satellite. Once it is in orbit, we should offer in good faith to turn over the information that it would get to the United Nations.

Lyndon Johnson ended his Senatorial career in 1960, when the Democratic Convention delegates nominated him for the Vice Presidency by acclamation.

8

☆

Vice President Johnson

Thousands of words have been written by political colum-
nists and analysts explaining why Lyndon Baines Johnson
was nominated as Vice Presidential candidate on the 1960
Democratic ticket. Brushing aside the haze of the smoke-
filled rooms where such decisions are traditionally made,
and the little noted incidents which assumed great signifi-
cance in later recollection, the reasons were probably two-
fold and possibly simple:

With the Presidential nomination secure in his own
pocket, John Fitzgerald Kennedy wanted a running mate
who could and would do the most to help him win the election. This was the man he had just beaten out as Presidential nominee.

Lyndon Johnson had learned party loyalty at the feet of
another President, Franklin D. Roosevelt. When asked by
Kennedy to accept the Vice Presidential nomination for
the good of the Democratic party, Johnson laid aside his
own bitter disappointment and accepted.

There were parallel reasons, of course. Kennedy respected Johnson as one of the most astute politicians of his time and as an honorable man. Both of these feelings Johnson returned in kind. And it is more than possible that Lyndon Johnson was looking for new worlds to conquer. As Senate Majority Leader he was often referred to as the second most powerful man in government. But Johnson had mastered that job as few men before him could. The thousand and one political strategies and details the Senate leadership involved had become second nature. A new field had its attractions. Reminded that other Vice Presidents had railed bitterly at the insignificance of the position, Johnson replied, "Power is where power goes."

Lyndon Johnson's major assignment during the 1960 campaign was to hold the conservative South for the Democratic ticket. This gave him two tough problems to overcome: Kennedy's Catholicism and Kennedy's position on Civil Rights. His campaign was not limited to the states below the Mason-Dixon line, but it was concentrated there.

He toured the land in a Lockheed Electra aircraft, outfitted for the purpose and dubbed "The Swoose—half swan, half goose," in memory of the old B–17 which had carried him throughout the Pacific in World War II days.

His strategy in the Southern states was clear and relatively simple. He talked of tolerance to the public crowds. He repeated again and again the story of how Joe Kennedy, Jr. (John Kennedy's older brother) and a Baptist minister had died fighting side by side in the war. He told his listeners that the Southern Negro had waited a hundred years for his freedom and "I think that's long enough, don't you?" He never deviated from the liberal party line and his respect for the views of the top man of the team.

Speaking in Richmond, Virginia, the former capital of

the Confederacy, he said, "I did not come down here to promise Virginia exemptions from the obligation to carry out the decisions of the Supreme Court (on civil rights)." Instead, he extended an invitation to "join the Union."

In private conferences with state political leaders, he told them to forget the platform and stick with the Democratic Party, for "We're going to win." It was effective. There were many of them who knew from his days as Majority Leader that having Lyndon Johnson as a political enemy could make the life of a politician unbearable.

To Northern labor Johnson gave assurances of his support for the things important to them—higher minimum wages, medical care for the aged under Social Security, Civil Rights and the liberalizing of labor laws. Labor believed him and carried the message to the industrial parts of the South where the Negro vote counted.

The Kennedy-Johnson ticket won by the closest popular vote in modern times, although with an electoral college plurality of 303 to 219. Most of the South went Democratic, including Lyndon Johnson's home state of Texas. It had gone Republican in the Presidential elections of both 1952 and 1956.

True to his faith in the man, President Kennedy gave Johnson a far greater role in the Executive Branch of the government than any previous Vice President had held. He was, by constitutional authority, President of the Senate. In addition, Kennedy asked him to attend all meetings of the Cabinet, provided for him an office in the White House Executive Office Building and named him: Member of the National Security Council, Chairman of the Peace Corps Advisory Committee, of the National Aeronautics and Space Council and of the President's Committee on Equal

Employment Opportunity. The Vice President, for example, participated in thirty-five meetings of the Security Council during the Cuban crisis in October, 1962.

However, it was to the two latter positions that the Vice President devoted most of his energy. The National Space Council had been established by Congress during the previous administration, in the same legislation which created the National Aeronautics and Space Administration (NASA), with its chairmanship designated for the President. President Eisenhower, who had not looked upon the exploration of space as particularly important, had never activated the Council.

Lyndon Johnson held an opposing view. His had been one of the urgent voices in Congress insisting that the United States must at all costs compete with Russia in the space race. As Chairman of the Preparedness Investigating Subcommittee of the Senate Armed Services Committee, he ordered and held an investigation immediately after the launching of Sputnik I, in October, 1957. One of the recommendations issued was for the immediate development of a million-pound thrust rocket.

Lyndon Johnson was Chairman of the Senate Select Committee, formed a few months later, which drafted the legislation creating NASA and the National Aeronautics and Space Council. He was the first Chairman of the National Aeronautics and Space Committee of the Senate.

During the 1960 campaign, President Kennedy had announced that, if elected, he would ask his Vice President to become Chairman of the Space Council. After the election Dr. Edward Welsh, an experienced Senate aide and advisor on military affairs, was named Executive Secretary of the Space Council, with an initial assignment of drafting legislation which would make the Vice President, instead of the President, the Chairman. This became law on April 25, 1961. Other authorized members of the Space Council are the Secretaries of State and Defense, the Director of the Budget, the Chairman of the Atomic Energy Commission, the President's Scientific Advisor and the Administrator of NASA.

Soon thereafter, President Kennedy wrote his Vice President, asking for an overall "crash" study to determine what was needed—and the cost—to accelerate the national space program. Johnson held a series of Council meetings. Dr. Welsh and NASA Administrator James E. Webb, with other Council members, worked night and day to come up at the deadline with a package proposal for what was needed, and the funds necessary. This was a fifty per cent increase in the old space program and President Kennedy presented it to a joint session of Congress in a special message on urgent national needs on May 25, 1961.

Among other points, it proposed the historic national goal of landing an American on the moon and returning him safely in this decade. Said President Kennedy:

"Now is the time to take longer strides—time for a great new American enterprise—time for this nation to take a clearly leading role in space achievement, which in many ways may hold the key to our future on earth.

"Recognizing the head start obtained by the Soviets," he continued, ". . . we nevertheless are required to make new efforts on our own. For while we cannot guarantee that we shall one day be first, we can guarantee that any failure to make this effort will make us last. . . . Space is open to us now; and our eagerness to share its meaning is not governed by the efforts of others. We go into space because whatever mankind must undertake, free men must fully share."

He asked Congress, at this time, to provide funds for several national space goals, including:

"First, I believe that this nation should commit itself to achieving the goal, before this decade is out, of landing a man on the moon and returning him safely to earth. No single space project in this period will be more impressive to mankind, or more important for the long-range exploration of space; and none will be more difficult or expensive to accomplish. . . . But in a very real sense, it will not be one man going to the moon—if we make this judgment affirmatively it will be an entire nation. For all of us must work to put him there."

Lyndon Johnson has said that he believes the country's advances in space exploration will be considered one of the outstanding achievements of the Kennedy administration.

During Johnson's Vice Presidency, meetings of the Space Council were held on call in his office in the White House Executive Office Building.

"The Council met, and still does, when there was business to be handled," said Dr. Welsh, who became acting Chairman of the Council when Johnson became President, as well as Executive Secretary. "Mr. Johnson is not a man to call meetings just to have meetings."

The Vice President, of course, presided. Defense Secretary McNamara always attended in person, according to Dr. Welsh, as did NASA Administrator Webb and AEC Chairman Glenn T. Seaborg. The fourth and only other member of the National Aeronautics and Space Council, Secretary of State Dean Rusk, occasionally was represented by Under Secretary George Ball, usually when Rusk was away from Washington.

The meetings were rarely long or windy. The Vice President was a forceful chairman and made his attitudes known to council members. There had been mistakes made in the past in the space program but there was no point in dwelling on them. With all of this nation's resources, we must achieve and maintain leadership.

"Mr. Johnson can't accept a 'no,'" said Dr. Welsh. "When he hears the word, he comes back with 'Why not? What do you need?'"

The President believes that the exploration of space is one of the more exciting and dynamic facets of our life today. He sees, also, benefits which will accrue from its stimulation on scientific progress—benefits to education and everyday living. He believes it is effective in international prestige and that space exploration can and should be a factor in world peace.

"He looks upon space as an arena in which no nation has charted out territory, where there is no room for nationalism," said Dr. Welsh.

The country took giant steps in space under the leadership of Lyndon Johnson. The first year, 1961, was the year of decision—decision to catch up with the Soviet space program and to put a man on the moon. The concrete action covered: a stepped-up big big rocket booster program, formulation of a satellite communications program, a general acceleration of individual space projects and doubling of the space budget.

The year 1962 saw the decisions of '61 being translated into action. Significant progress was made in manned earth-orbiting flight. Astronaut John Glenn made the first American orbital flight on February 20, followed by Scott Carpenter and Walter Schirra. During that year, the United States put more than fifty satellite payloads in orbit to collect space information in the fields of meteorology, geodesy, navigation and communication. The quasi-public Communications Satellite Corporation was formed.

In reporting on the space program for 1963, the Chairman wrote:

"The National Aeronautics and Space Council has been guided by the premise that the United States will become the world's leading spacefaring nation and that it will dedicate its space competence to improving and maintaining the peace. To this end, our national space program has been designed to increase our knowledge of the space environment and the fundamental facts of nature; to master the technology of manned and unmanned space flight; to explore the solar system; to increase our national security; and to utilize the results of space technology and discovery to achieve a broad range of economic and social benefits.

"Our goals include increased international cooperation in the use of outer space for peaceful purposes, the development of the regime of law for outer space and the orderly and open conduct of space-related activities."

The year, 1963, saw Astronaut Leroy Gordon Cooper complete a 34-orbit flight to close out the Mercury project, the launching of the world's first synchronous satellite and of the world's first all-nuclear-powered satellite and the first orbiting of a nuclear test detection satellite.

In an allied, although different field, the Space Council formulated and recommended to President Kennedy that the United States initiate a supersonic transport prototype development program at the earliest possible date. The

President accepted the recommendation and United States industry was invited to submit proposals for an airliner which would fly in excess of 2,000 miles an hour.

It would be wrong, probably, to say that Lyndon Johnson considered the space program any less important than his other major interest as Vice President, the President's Committee for Equal Employment Opportunity. It is more likely that he realized the space program, once directed toward its goal and under way, would progress through its own momentum. Contrarily, the PCEEO demanded his personal attention and energy because of the controversial nature and complexity of the problem. Certainly the task of eliminating discrimination in jobs became his major day-to-day activity.

Within his first one hundred days as President, the late John Kennedy signed Executive Order 10925—on March 6, 1961—establishing the Committee and naming the Vice President as Chairman. In signing it, President Kennedy said:

"Denial of the right to work is unfair, regardless of its victim. It is doubly unfair to throw its burden on someone because of his race or color."

The order put the government's economic power squarely into the forefront of the administration's campaign to obtain equal opportunity in both employment and job promotion. It directed the Committee to scrutinize employment practices of the Government of the United States and to recommend any necessary steps to stop inequities. It decreed that all private industry when engaged on government contracts must maintain nondiscriminatory employment and promotion policies, and it provided sanctions and cancellation penalties. The order directed the Com-

mittee to "use its best offorts" through "all available instru-
mentalities" to see that labor unions complied with the
spirit of the President's order.

The Vice President's first action as Chairman of the
PCEEO came less than a month after the Committee's
formation. Complaints of job discrimination were received
concerning the Lockheed Aircraft Corporation, at Marietta, Georgia. Out of a series of conferences between Committee members and Lockheed's management came the first
Plan for Progress. It covered not only Lockheed Marietta
but all of the company's corporate facilities. This first Plan
for Progress was signed in the White House on May 25,
1961, by Vice President Johnson and Lockheed President
Courtlandt S. Gross. President Kennedy witnessed the
signing.

Even while the Lockheed negotiations were under way,
the Vice President called a meeting of the Presidents of the
fifty largest government contractors. He asked—and obtained—from them pledges that they would cooperate in
fighting discrimination in employment and job advancement. Most of these firms later signed Plans for Progress.

It was typical of Lyndon Johnson, in evolving the Plan
for Progress, that he chose the road of voluntary cooperation rather than that of shotgun enforcement. Since his
earliest political days, the Vice President had always leaned
heavily on the art of persuasion as the most logical way to
victory.

The Plan for Progress scheme had one tremendous ad-
vantage over an involuntary method. It permitted Johnson
and the Committee to enroll members who were not government contractors and over whom the Committee held
no power or threat for enforcement, to achieve fair hiring

practices. Getting this voluntary cooperation was probably the greatest single accomplishment of the Committee.

There was an important point also in placing the acquiescence of government contractors on a voluntary basis. Although Johnson had the enforcement clause to back up his hand, cancellation of a government contract is not a simple thing. It can involve millions of dollars of expenditure and months or even years of development work already accomplished.

"We haven't cancelled any contracts," said the Vice President, after he had been Chairman for nearly two years. (None, in fact, were cancelled during his entire tenure.) "But, we have informed officials many times that we were about to cancel. We have adjudicated some five hundred or more cases and seventy-three per cent were decided in favor of the complainant, the person who complained he was being discriminated against."

Signers of the Plans for Progress are relieved of none of the responsibilities inherent in the Executive Order. Complaints against them are processed and investigated in the same manner as against all others. The Plans for Progress does make compliance easier and more palatable.

Specifically, the signers agree to: seek out aggressively qualified Negro candidates for technical, mechanical and clerical jobs; inform college placement officials of company policies and request referral of qualified Negroes; review personnel records of the company to insure Negroes are both fairly compensated and considered for advancement; provide training to permit advancement of Negroes; insure that layoffs are nondiscriminatory; maintain company facilities on a desegregated basis.

Plans for Progress members also participate in the exchange of employment ideas with other members, and in studies. The Committee, through recruitment, training and labor liaison programs, helps them find qualified workers.

By the Committee's first anniversary in 1962, fifty-two of the country's largest corporations had signed Plans for Progress. By early 1964, the number had grown to 115, including many companies which do not hold government contracts. Nineteen top industrial executives had formed a special Advisory Council to aid the program.

Simultaneous with the industry side of the PCEEO program came the Union Program for Fair Practices, initiated to crack the labor problem, which is described in a Committee report:

"The problem of securing equal employment opportunity is not confined to any single industry or union, to any type of industry or union, or to any part of the country. In all the many subdivisions of commerce and industry, employment patterns have generally tended to restrict various minority groups from time to time—and Negroes most of the time—to semiskilled, seasonal and laborer or service classifications."

In recognition of this, and other inequalities of labor practices, leaders of the American Federation of Labor-Committee of Industrial Organization and one hundred and fifteen international unions affiliated with the AFL-CIO, met at the White House with Vice President Johnson, on November 15, 1962. There, the major portion of American organized labor, with a membership of some eleven million workers, pledged to speed up its program to insure equal opportunity in union membership, union facilities and all other aspects of union employment.

In addition, AFL-CIO President George Meany named a special committee to work with local unions throughout the country to help "wipe out discrimination wherever it exists—on the jobs, in the schools, in the voting booth, in the housing developments, stores, theaters or recreation areas."

In the meantime, of course, the government had to put its own house in order. It could hardly point an accusing finger at industry and labor when its own federal employment roles reflected some, if possibly not as much, discrimination.

A survey made in the spring of 1961 established that most government Negro employees were concentrated in the lower grades; that relatively few reached the upper levels.

The Committee organized a series of regional meetings with leaders of federal agencies in the field, one in each of the fourteen Civil Service regions. The meetings were followed by across-the-table conferences between committee members and regional agency chiefs and personnel chiefs.

A second survey (1962) noted some improvement and a report for 1963 was considerably better. In government jobs paying from $9,475 to $20,000, for example, 1963 showed a gain of 545 more Negroes employed than 1962, a gain of 38.7 per cent. (The overall national increase in this category was 12.4 per cent.) Total employment of nonwhites had gained greatly. Similar surveys will be made annually.

In all of the labors of Vice President Johnson's Committee, from all the surveys, conferences and reports, one fact emerges with constant clarity—that the economic condition of the Negro and, to some extent, other minority groups, is due to a syndrome which must be changed before any real permanent cure for discrimination can be effected.

Put very simply, the economic position of many minority group families is so depressed that their children are neither educated nor trained well enough to compete for higher-paying jobs; and, without the higher income these better jobs will provide, they will not be educated and trained sufficiently to qualify for the good positions. It is a vicious circle.

In a major Southern industrial city, for example, a government contractor wanted to hire Negro secretaries and clerical workers. Tests were given to all members of the graduating commercial class in the local all-Negro high school. One girl passed the aptitude test; another passed the performance test. No one of the Negro girls passed both tests.

It was then decided to check the teacher. She failed both exams.

It was with a full understanding of this inequality of teacher standards that the Vice President welcomed into the Plans for Progress family its first educational institution member—Wayne State University of Detroit, in July, 1963.

In signing, Wayne State officials noted that the University prohibits any form of discrimination in admission, advancement, housing, educational services or athletic competition.

More, at the instigation of Wayne State, a conference was held in Ann Arbor, Michigan, on October 21, 1962. Attending were all of the Big Ten Universities and the University of Chicago. Together they represented some 350,000 students.

It was, said Lyndon Johnson, the real beginning behind the mobilization of the educational and intellectual forces of the nation behind the government's cooperative program for improving the opportunities of minority group citizens on a broad scale.

The Big Ten schools and Chicago University indicated they would join Wayne State in the program. One project favorably considered at the conference was that each university would adopt a "sister" Negro school, in the South or elsewhere, to exchange students and faculties and for various cultural activities.

Meetings of the President's Committee on Equal Employment Opportunities are held in the Executive Office Building. Committee members include the Secretaries of Labor (Vice Chairman), Commerce, Health, Education and Welfare, and Defense, the Attorney General, the three Service Secretaries, the Administrators of NASA and the AEC, and a number of private citizens. One of the latter is Walter Reuther, the labor leader.

In presiding over these meetings, the Vice President demonstrated in various ways his skill at handling people and situations. On one occasion he was commenting on the employment situation at Huntsville, Alabama, among the nation's great space centers. Said the Vice President:

"Here is one of the top communities in the nation from the standpoint of Government employment. Twenty per cent of the community is non-white and only three per cent of the non-whites are employed. . . . This is a reasonable indication that there is either lack of skill or qualification or (that there is) discrimination or the figures wouldn't be so widely separated."

Walter Reuther brought up the point that other factors,

such as unfavorable housing or living conditions, might be the cause and not a lack of qualification—that perhaps well-qualified Negroes would not care to live in Huntsville, Alabama. He ended by asking:

"Why does the Government pursue a policy whereby it continues to locate many of these defense contracts in areas where the existing social pattern is such that it is difficult (for a Negro to live)?"

"There are not many parts of America where we don't have the same problem, Walter, if you want to be candid about it," replied the Vice President.

On another occasion, Attorney General Robert Kennedy and NASA Administrator James Webb clashed with some acrimony. The Vice President had just pointed out that the Plans for Progress agreements "contain substantially more affirmative efforts than the (Presidential) order requires. The order prohibits discrimination, but the agreement itself obligates the contractor to do considerably more than that and he agrees to do it voluntarily."

This was followed by a discussion which brought out the fact that surveys of various companies by the government contracting agencies to see that these obligations were being carried out were proceeding slowly.

The Attorney General, whose department does not engage in outside contracting, was questioning this slowness and asking about the number of persons each agency had working on the project. The Department of Defense reported some fifty employed on survey work, and AEC named eight. The following exchange then took place, regarding NASA.

Attorney General: "Could I ask, Mr. Webb, how many people do you have working on your program?"

Mr. Webb: "Let me ask Mr. Hartson (an aide)."

The Attorney General: "Who is the head—?"

Mr. Webb: "Mr. Hartson is following this continuously. Will you answer the Attorney General's question?"

Mr. Hartson: "We have one and a half man years of full-time effort in the headquarters and we have efforts carried out through both personnel offices and procurement offices in the field."

The Attorney General: "What is one and a half years?"

Mr. Hartson: "One year of a man full time in the office of procurement doing nothing but this. The other half man year is me."

The Attorney General: "What is the value of your government contracts?"

Mr. Hartson: "It is about ninety per cent of $3.47 billion."

The Attorney General: "And you can do that with one and a half men per year?"

There followed several minutes of sharply skeptical questions from Attorney General Kennedy, the President's brother. When this had gone on as long as he felt it should, the Chairman stepped in like any good umpire.

"Mr. Attorney General," Johnson said quietly, "we of the Committee have met with the leading agencies who have the most contracts, namely the Department of Defense, General Services Administration, the Post Office Department, the Veterans Administration and the Space Agency. We have asked them to undertake compliance surveys of the companies under their jurisdiction.

"Now as an illustration of what is happening today," he continued, "the Space Agency is investigating a company (he named a California firm) that has a contract with us.

Mr. Webb doesn't do the investigating . . . any more than you would try a case in California for the Department of Justice. You have a district attorney for that, just as NASA looks to its Division Director to see that this order is enforced."

On one occasion at least, the Vice President harked back to his NYA days in Texas. He told the committee:

"Even if you solved all the discrimination in employment tomorrow, other discrimination that has existed over the years in education, in housing and in association has yet to be dealt with.

"Just look at your employment rolls," he continued. "We have almost a million Negroes on them and the training and skills they have reflect the discrimination that has existed all these years in education. While we don't want to institute anything like leaf raking in the program, the thing we are really going to have to face up to is: Aren't we going to have to develop some kind of a program that will permit unskilled people and illiterate people to find some way to employ their talents and earn by work rather than be supported by welfare?"

Then, thinking back to 1935, when he was first named director of the National Youth Administration for Texas, he said:

"Back in the depression years, Mr. Hopkins (Harry Hopkins was an assistant to President Roosevelt) sent me a wire and asked, 'How many people are you going to have working by next Saturday night?' "

The young administrator had been on the job only a few days. "We had very little (money) for material and very little for supervision, and it is not good business to employ a man without adequate supervision or without his doing something worthwhile," Johnson explained. "So we went to the State Highway Department and we said, 'You have had many things you couldn't do all through the years because of limited resources, but if we will assign you fifteen thousand men and we will pay their salaries twice a month —they are unskilled men—will you give them top flight supervision and built-in organization—not to supplant somebody but to supplement someone?' They said, 'Yes.'

"So we wired back, 'We will have fifteen thousand assigned.'

"They took those people (jobless Texas youngsters) and a good many of them are now in our highway system, some of them as bulldozer operators, some as maintenance men, some as tractor operators, because of that training. It may be that we ought to consider . . . some kind of a program that will have more substance to it than raking leaves, but won't require any greater skill . . . where they (the unemployed) can in dignity go out and earn their own pay check, instead of getting it in the form of a welfare payment."

The Executive Vice President of the President's Committee on Equal Employment Opportunities is Hobart Taylor, a Negro attorney from Detroit but who was born and received his early education in Texas. Taylor actively supported Lyndon Johnson's bid for the Presidency in 1960 and, after being elected Vice President, Johnson arranged to have Taylor named special counsel for the PEECO. From that position he eventually moved on up to the Vice Chairmanship.

Of Lyndon Johnson's accomplishments as Chairman of the Committee, Taylor said:

"There has been a basic change in attitude on the part of most of the managers of American industry and the heads of our responsible labor unions. For the first time, these leaders of private industry have undertaken a rigorous self-scrutiny to determine their true attitudes. For the first time there is under way in our nation today an intensive examination of new human resources."

"The leadership of Mr. Johnson," declared Taylor, "has been very personal. He has attended meeting after meeting. He has made speeches and talked personally with leaders of both industry and labor. And he has made both labor and industry conscious of discrimination, both from an economic and a human point of view. He has turned their thinking around."

9

☆

America's Traveling Ambassador

At sprawling Andrews Air Force Base in Maryland, a few miles from the nation's capital, four sleek long-range jet aircraft are stabled and cared for like entries in the Kentucky Derby.

They are VC–137 models, luxury versions of the Boeing 707 passenger liners. The "C" stands for "Cargo." The "V" stands for "VIP"—Very Important Person. These four are the fast, much-used nucleus of the "Presidential Fleet," which carries the President, Vice President, Cabinet Members and sometimes members of Congress on official missions around the world.

Newest of the four VC–137s is the one reserved especially for Lyndon Johnson.

All four of the big airliners are designed as conference planes—flying offices. The older three have roughly the same configuration. They will carry about fifty passengers each. The fuselage is divided into three compartments. Up front are simply regulation seats. The mid-section has working desks, conference tables and one sofa. The rear section is equipped with more elegant and comfortable chairs and desks, and two sofas. All three of the sofas make up into beds.

The fourth and newest of the C–137s was originally ordered for President Kennedy, with some interior design suggestions, it is said, from Mrs. Jacqueline Kennedy. It will seat fewer passengers in more comfort and with greater working space than the other three aircraft. It has a bedroom compartment finished in blue which will sleep as many as six. A private office is walnut-panelled, with furnishings that are distinctly "executive." There are a television and other amenities.

Officially, the Presidential Fleet is the 1254 USAF Air Transport Wing, and the planes are United States Air Force Special Mission (SAM) aircraft. The SAM Wing also has two dozen or more other aircraft—Connies, Aero-Commanders, DC–6s, Convair Liners and Jet Stars. On short flights within this country, the President usually flies in one of the Jet Stars or perhaps an Aero-Commander. Any USAF aircraft the President is using automatically becomes USAF One, in Air Force records.

As a Senator, Lyndon Johnson was not unfamiliar with the SAM planes. As Vice President, the big VC–137s became almost a second home. During the thirty-seven months he served as the nation's number two man he traveled some 111,000 miles and visited thirty countries, in twenty-four of which he made a total of 150 speeches and was seen by literally millions of people.

(During these thirty-seven months, incidentally, he also appeared in thirty-five of the United States, where he made 186 addresses—plus 193 in the District of Columbia.)

While he was still the Senator from Massachusetts, the

late John F. Kennedy once remarked to friends that Lyndon Johnson was probably the best qualified man in the United States to be President.

In selecting Johnson for his running mate in 1960, Kennedy said that he wanted "a man who cared" and that Lyndon Johnson did.

There were political reasons, of course, but, in light of later events, they do not seem as important as those earlier two Kennedy named. Once in office, he appeared to set out on a deliberate course to instruct Johnson as an understudy in the exacting assignments of the Presidency—ready for a day neither expected to come.

If Johnson was unhappy in the second spot—and there were many of his friends who felt that he chafed under the limitations and restrictions of the office—he never remotely indicated the fact in public. There was no backbiting, no complaining. He accepted his tasks and threw the weight of the famous Johnson energy into them. In most assignments he was well qualified, and he was also prepared for the many behind-the-scene chores he performed on the administration's behalf with Congress. These were in a field he knew well—domestic problems and domestic politics.

In another area, international affairs, he was less prepared and less qualified. During his service in Congress, both as a Representative and a Senator, he was more frequently absorbed by domestic affairs than by foreign. As Senate Majority Leader, Johnson was often called upon to rescue a foreign aid bill from the massacre of his colleagues, but he did it more as part of his job and because of party loyalty than because he held, at that time, the same strong convictions on foreign aid that he was later to acquire.

Primarily, Lyndon Johnson was a Texan, with much of the insularity common to the Lone Star State. Consequently, when President Kennedy called upon him to act as his special envoy on a number of international missions —a deliberate move to school him in this field, many believe—the Vice President found himself boning up in a new area of politics.

He did his homework well. He had briefings prepared on the countries he would visit, the people, their cultures and economics, and he studied them carefully. He spent serious hours on protocol, customs and taboos. (Europeans shake hands; Asians usually do not.)

Johnson's first foreign assignment was on April 3, 1961, just six weeks after the inauguration. President Kennedy sent him as personal representative to the ceremonies marking the independence of the Republic of Senegal, formerly part of French West Africa, on the Atlantic Ocean.

En route home from Senegal's capital of Dakar, Johnson stopped off in Geneva, Switzerland, where three-power talks were under way on the nuclear test ban treaty. After a briefing here on the United States position and progress of the negotiations, Johnson continued on by jet to Paris, to represent President Kennedy at the tenth anniversary of Supreme Headquarters, Allied Powers, Europe— SHAPE.

In May of 1961, President Kennedy tapped Johnson for another foreign mission, this time to southern and southeast Asia, to reassure friendly nations there of continued aid and support from the United States. This 29,000-mile journey took the Vice President officially to Viet-Nam, the Philippines, the Republic of China, the Crown Colony of Hong Kong, Thailand, India and Pakistan.

En route, there were other and unofficial stops of varying duration—mostly for refueling—at Honolulu, Wake, Guam, Formosa, Bangkok, and Athens. Accompanying Lyndon Johnson on the trip were Mrs. Johnson, President Kennedy's sister, Jean, and her husband, Stephen Smith.

The uneasy political situation in Viet-Nam was one of the compelling causes of the trip, and Saigon was the first official stop. Truce negotiations to end the guerilla fighting with the Viet Cong forces had stalled and the jungle warfare itself was drearily inconclusive. In Saigon, where some two years later a revolt would bring about the deposition and murder the nation's President, Johnson addressed the Republic of Viet-Nam's National Assembly. He told its members:

"I have informed your President that the United States is ready to assist South Viet-Nam in coping with the grave situation with which it is confronted. There are many things which the United States is willing to do, including taking steps toward improving South Viet-Nam's capacity to resist the subversive and terrorist maneuvers of the Communist guerillas."

The Vice President's program, in addition to increasing military strength, covered aid to education, establishment of new industries, and general long-term economic development.

While Johnson drove through the May heat from the airport to the Palace in Saigon, where the visitors from the United States were to stay, he was cheered by thousands of people who lined the road into the city. When he left Saigon, the crowds were even greater and, as his party proceeded, temptation was too much for the Texas politician. He stopped, got out of the car and walked into the throng, shaking hands, and asking and answering questions through his interpreter.

In Manila, the next stop on the tour, Johnson reviewed the honor guard, then again plunged into the crowd to shake hundreds of hands, chatting, smiling, projecting Lyndon Johnson. He continued this at the other stops during his journey.

There were conflicting opinions after Johnson's return as to the success of his trip and the effect of his people-to-people diplomacy. It wasn't prescribed, it wasn't usual. He spent more time with the public than with the officials. Often, schedules had to be revised because of the delays he caused with his unscheduled stops along the route.

But one thing is certain. With every stop, the crowds increased and so did the cheers. At the end of the journey, Johnson remarked that never once during the trip had he seen an unfriendly face or heard a hostile voice.

In Manila, he was met by the Philippine Republic's President, Carlos P. Garcia. Addressing a joint session of the Philippine Congress, he told its members that the cold war against Communism in Asia could be won only by giving the people something to believe in and to fight for. "America will continue in the future to march along with you in the war against poverty, illiteracy, disease, and other social blights," he said.

From Manila, the Vice President's big VC–137 jet took him and his party to Formosa, where he conferred with President Chang Kai-Shek. He reassured the aging Generalissimo and Madame Chang that the United States will never abandon Formosa to recognize Red China.

From there, Johnson went to Hong Kong and then flew on to Bangkok, in Thailand. He told Thailand's Prime

Minister, Field Marshal Sarit Thanarat, that the policy of the Kennedy administration toward southeast Asia is based on the "moral, legal and spiritual pledge to defend the unity, integrity and independence of that ancient land against Chinese Communism." The two men had a five-hour conversation covering the effectiveness of SEATO (Southeast Asia Treaty Organization) and American policies in that area. Johnson assured the Prime Minister that, in the absence of adequate protection from SEATO, the United States would adopt an independent policy for strengthening the defense of Thailand.

The United States party left Bangkok, someone noted, with a memory of elephants and golden horns, jade cupolas, tiny emerald statues, barefoot children, and oppressive heat.

Johnson's talks with Indian Prime Minister Nehru, in New Delhi, the next stop, were focused almost exclusively on economic problems and American economic aid.

Johnson told newsmen: "We talked of Mr. Nehru's hopes and aspirations and of our desire to help. The common enemies of mankind on which a major attack must be mounted are ignorance, poverty and disease." He placed a wreath on the spot where Gandhi was cremated.

From New Delhi, Johnson flew to Karachi for a twenty-four hour visit with Marshal Ayub, President of Pakistan, and told him:

"When starting out on this trip, I said that it was a mission of faith that peace and freedom will prevail. At each stage of the trip, this faith has been strengthened by the high character of responsibility and by the determined will I have found everywhere to serve the cause of peace and freedom."

Here, as in the other countries he had visited, Johnson found the crowds that lined the streets were more interesting than the high officials, although he must have found the scene there far different from that of distant Texas.

The only non-American correspondent who accompanied this Vice Presidential trip, Ilario Fiore of the Milan newspaper *Il Tempo,* wrote of one street scene in Karachi:

"At the market place of Korgani are the thousands of barefoot children in the inexorable whiteness, the white heat of a Sunday afternoon in summer. It is a crowd of the poor. When we stop and get out they try to kiss the hand of Kennedy's sister, Jean, while they sing a song of love. They cry out the name of Kashmir in hoarse voices, with a remote note of bitterness."

One of the people Johnson met among the street crowds in Karachi was a camel driver named Bashir Ahmid. The tall American talked with him at length and, as he moved on, said, "Come and visit me sometime." Lyndon Johnson probably never in his life issued an invitation he was more surprised to have accepted!

The far eastern mission of the Vice President ended with an overnight stop in Athens and he returned to the United States the next morning.

Word of the friendly encounter of the American Vice President and the Pakistani camel driver got around after Johnson's return home. Just where the move started is obscure, but, within a few weeks, a group of American businessmen, it is said, began working on the project through the People-to-People program in the State Department, and that fall, Bashir Ahmid sent word he was accepting the Vice President's invitation to visit him.

Bashir began his trip from Karachi in mid-October,

1961, by arising at dawn and downing strong tea in preparation for his first airplane flight. His wife, Chidoo, his four children, brother-in-law, and three neighbor women saw him off at the airport. Normally, Bashir wore a shirt, turban and two and a half yards of cloth draped around his waist and legs. For the trip to America, he wore a "Jinnah" fur cap, a long coat known as a "sherwani" and flowing baggy trousers called "shilwar." And, for the first time in his life, he wore shoes.

Lyndon Johnson met Bashir at Idlewild Airport, in New York, and was, one reporter wrote, "pale and apprehensive" as he watched the small, wiry figure—his guest—walk down the ramp, "with a smile as wide as his handlebar mustache."

If Johnson was concerned about the social refinements of his unusual guest, it was without cause. Bashir was a camel driver. He was also a poet whose quotations were so graceful the interpreter had trouble matching them in English, and his demeanor was impeccable. He charmed everyone who met him, including the nation's press.

To Lyndon Johnson's apology for the cold weather, he replied, "It is not the cold; it is the warmth of people's hearts that matters."

From Idlewild the Vice President took the camel driver to the LBJ Ranch at Johnson City, where Bashir looked things over from the saddle of a prize quarter-horse—which he thought might be a fair trade for a camel. (Value of a camel: $150. Value of the quarterhorse: $500.)

The first words of English Bashir learned were "so long," which he used when he left with the Vice President for Dallas after a two-day visit at the ranch. On the way from the airport he inspected a supermarket and was chiefly amazed at the door which opened by photoelectric cell. He saw the sights of the State Fair of Texas, in Dallas, and there was surprised with a present of a truck, donated by the Ford Motor Company. It was blue. Bashir preferred green, so it was exchanged for a green one.

On the evening of October 17, Bashir flew to Independence, Missouri, where President Truman found his manners so courtly he flusteredly called his guest "Your Excellency" at one point. At the Truman Library, his host gave the camel driver a good luck charm, and later took him to the auction of a prize steer, and served him a steak breakfast.

In Washington, Bashir was taken on a tour of the Capitol by Mrs. Johnson. On meeting her, he said:

"Words drop from your lips like the petals of a flower."

Of the Johnson girls, he told their father:

"A daughter in the family is like spring among the seasons." Bashir had affectionate words for his own four sons and one daughter, and for his camel, which apparently was mean but lovable.

Mrs. Johnson took Bashir to the Islamic Center, where he properly removed his shoes. He had lunch at the Pakistan Embassy, visited the Lincoln Memorial, the Capitol, and the James Madison High School, in Vienna, Virginia. At the White House, President Kennedy saw him being shown about and called him in for a brief chat. In New York, during the night of October 20, the camel driver stayed in a forty-five-dollar suite at the Waldorf Astoria, after visiting the United Nations building, the Statue of Liberty, and the Staten Island ferry.

Informed by a newsman that his wife, back in Karachi,

had reportedly moved from their family hut into an apartment, he said:

"A woman is like a camel. You never know what she will do next."

As he was preparing to leave the United States for home, Bashir received a telegram from his friend, the Vice President. It read: "Since your return to Pakistan takes you so close to Mecca, arrangements have been made through the People-to-People program for you to visit there."

"Allah be praised!" cried Bashir, and burst into tears.

While Johnson's trip to the Far East had been primarily political, it produced a fair measure of fallout benefits from the Vice President's practiced observations. Soon after his return he sought a meeting with Defense Secretary Robert McNamara, his top aides, the Service Secretaries and military Chiefs of Staff. He gave them his ideas concerning the activities of military missions in the various countries he had visited; he dwelt particularly on the relations of the military with the civilian diplomatic staffs. He suggested that budget experts be named to each country to correlate foreign spending with actual appropriations and the rate at which such funds were to be spent.

Johnson brought back to President Kennedy Pakistan President Ayub's proposals for increased United States aid for checking the salinity and water-logging of Pakistan's farm lands. His report resulted in a scientific mission being sent from this country to study the problem and draw up a plan for joint action. Dr. Jerome B. Wiesner, the President's Scientific Advisor, headed the mission.

For a more utilitarian dividend, the Vice President dug deep into his memories of his youth in Johnson City. While visiting an Indian village, he recalled that, long before the present network of lines brought electricity to his home town in Texas, electric power was produced by kerosene-run generators.

He saw no reason why these would not work as well in India and, on his return, learned that the same kerosene units were still in production. Today, they are being used in a test project for pumping water and lighting in rural India.

Whether or not Lyndon Johnson needed converting to the idea, there is little doubt in the minds of his colleagues that he returned from these first two "educational" trips assigned by President Kennedy a confirmed believer in the cause of foreign aid. He reported these convictions in a speech at the National Press Club in Washington, D. C., and in greater detail to the Senate Foreign Relations Committee. He was a zealot, he said, "in the conviction that the tide of history can be turned in our cause of freedom."

President Kennedy next asked Johnson to undertake a mission to Germany, for personal discussions with then German Chancellor Konrad Adenauer and Berlin's Mayor Willy Brandt on the Berlin situation. Earlier that year, Johnson had entertained Adenauer at the LBJ ranch.

"Welcome to Texas," he said as the old German Chancellor stepped from the plane on the LBJ runway. Three years later, he would have said, "Welcome to the United States," just as three years later only two flags flew over the LBJ ranch—the American flag and President's. The Lone Star flag of Texas had gone. As President, Lyndon Johnson had become a citizen of the United States—not of Texas.

He entertained Adenauer with a choral group from New Braunfels singing German songs, readily familiar to this German-American community. And, he staged an ox roast in the nearby village of Stonewall, for the ramrod erect old foreign politician.

By August, 1961, the Soviet government had become alarmed to the point of action over the steady and continued flight of East Germans to the West. The action came in the form of a concrete and barbed wire "Wall" separating West Berlin from East and the cutting off of all normal communication between the two parts of the German city.

Fearing for the morale of the West Berliners and the possible flight of capital business and residents, Mayor Willy Brandt sent an urgent note to President Kennedy. The White House reaction was to dispatch Vice President Johnson, with General Lucius D. Clay (former American commander in Berlin) and State Department Soviet expert Charles Bohlen, on a weekend mission to reassure our late enemies of World War II. Kennedy also ordered fifteen hundred additional American troops in to reinforce the Berlin garrison.

Johnson took his official party down the autobahn to greet the incoming soldiers, toured West Berlin, visited the "Wall" and was seen and heard by a million or more West Germans. On a dozen occasions he left his car to plunge into the crowds, shaking hands, passing out ball point pens bearing his name and gilt-edge cards of admission to the Vice President's gallery in the Senate. The visit was not a cure for the basic situation in Berlin, nor was it expected to be, but it was successful in that it boosted the sagging morale of the West Germans as nothing else might have. It also enhanced the reputation of Lyndon Johnson.

September of that same year saw Johnson in Sweden, representing President Kennedy at the funeral of United Nations Secretary-General Dag Hammarskjold. In August of 1962, he made two trips: the first to Jamaica in the Caribbean, celebrating its independence that August 6; the second to Lebanon, Iran, Turkey, Cyprus and Greece.

In Beirut, Lebanon, Johnson assured the people that the United States had an "abiding and unchanging interest in the independence and integrity of Lebanon." He was mindful of the fact that the United States had helped assure free elections there in 1958 by landing marines.

In Teheran, Iran, the Vice President greeted the Monarch, Shah Mohammed Reza Rahlavi, as an old friend who had visited Washington and told him, "A free Iran is vital to the strength of the free world. Iran's independence and national integrity will not be breached."

The pledges of the Truman Doctrine which helped prevent Turkey from falling behind the Iron Curtain after World War II were renewed at Ankara.

Departing Cyprus, Johnson told a crowd that he left "with certainty that Cyprus and the United States enjoy the understanding and mutual trust of friends dedicated to freedom." In Athens he placed assurances of the continuance of foreign aid.

The Johnson party on this trip included Mrs. Johnson and their elder daughter, Lynda Bird, who left the official party at Athens, accompanied by a chaperone, to keep a date with a Naval officer—a friend of long standing—whose ship was in Italy. Throughout the trip, the Vice President maintained the tradition he had started on earlier foreign journeys; he spent more time with the people than with the political leaders.

Driving from the airport in Beirut, he stopped the motorcade to chat with a boy melon vendor. Later, he delayed the party to talk with Palestine refugees at a refugee settlement. At a road construction project (started with American aid but by then self-sustaining), Johnson climbed up on bulldozers and trucks to inspect the progress of the work, and noted that his first job out of high school in Texas had been with a road-building crew.

He shook hundreds of hands when a crowd estimated at 225,000 gathered to meet him in Teheran. Later, wearing a sport shirt and slacks, he drove in an open car through the poorer sections of the city, stopping to talk with the residents. It was hot and perspiration dripped from his forehead. In the Turkish sector of Nicosia, Cyprus, he joined and danced in the street with a dozen lovely Turkish girls. Greek school children from a farm school gave him a baby donkey and he in return presented the school with a new tractor from the American government.

On September 2, 1963, the Vice President left the United States, again with Mrs. Johnson and their daughter Lynda Bird, on a journey to the five Nordic nations of Sweden, Finland, Norway, Denmark and Iceland, a trip of some fifteen thousand miles. With the heads of state of each nation visited, the Vice President carried out discussions primarily concerned with new lines of world trade, including the relationship of the United States to the Common Market of Europe. Mrs. Johnson, equally goodwill-bent, visited typical farms and co-operatives, and met with women leaders of the countries.

In Sweden, the Vice President lunched with King Gustaf Adolf VI and had a narrow escape from injury when the landing gear of his helicopter hooked a fence but the aircraft landed safely. Outside his hotel, he chatted with an elderly taxi driver who could not understand why "that nice man walked up and shook hands." He signed hundreds of autographs.

In Helsinki, Finland, Johnson's hosts were embarrassed by two eggs hurled from a crowd. They splashed harmlessly against a window and the Vice President did not even see them. He flew over the Arctic Circle to Lapland and spent most of a day in the rather stark countryside near Rovaniemi, where three thousand Finns and Lapps at the airport, and thousands more in town, gathered to greet him. Driving in from the airport, he made several stops to chat with farm workers and at one Lynda Bird was surrounded by a flock of youngsters. When a Secret Service man suggested she hurry, the Vice President's daughter told him:

"Listen, you tell Daddy he got me into this and I can't get out in a hurry."

In a Helsinki market place Johnson had an unplanned meeting with Paavo Nurmi, the "Flying Finn" of the 1920s, holder of seven Olympic gold medals. He invited the famous distance runner to visit him in Washington, which Nurmi did, early in 1964, after Johnson became President.

In Copenhagen, the Vice President found an old friend of the Johnson family, a second generation Danish-American boy who had been a Senate page and who was studying at the University of Copenhagen. He joined the official party for the duration of their visit there. The crowds in the Danish capital were so great the police could not control the traffic and the special motorcade was delayed twelve minutes on the trip from airport to hotel. Later, in Copenhagen's midtown amusement ground, enchanting Tivoli, the President and other members of the family got completely lost from the official party. Lynda Bird was presented with a Greenlander costume and happily posed in it for photographers.

Lyndon Johnson's last trip abroad as Vice President was to the Benelux Countries—Belgium, the Netherlands and Luxembourg—in early November, 1963. His primary objective was for discussions on the European Coal and Steel Community, and to deliver an address to the Netherlands-American Institute at The Hague.\Mr. and Mrs. Johnson were received by three of the remaining monarchs of Europe—the Grand Duchess of Luxembourg, the Queen of the Netherlands and the King of Belgium. The Vice President's party received its most enthusiastic reception in the one-thousand-year-old Duchy of Luxembourg, which, the press noted, was smaller than some of the ranches in Johnson's native Texas.

When the assassination of President Kennedy thrust Johnson into the Presidency on November 22, 1963, and when he had accomplished the delicate transition of power in the White House, the Texan moved with deliberate force on the Kennedy legislative program. But it would have been unthinkable of the new President to continue under the mantle of his predecessor and to wear any longer the label of the Kennedy New Frontier.

The concept of the new administration had the ring of good, sound politics. But it might as honestly have had its roots in his own life history: in the have-not days of his Texas youth; in his narrow escape from being himself a school dropout; in the penny-stretching frustrations of the NYA during the Great Depression; or even from his reflections on the mass hunger of the thousands who cheered him blindly on his journey through Asia. The new concept was the Great Society.

10

☆

The Great Society

The Spring of 1966 saw Lyndon Johnson well into his third year of the Presidency. In the eyes of the majority of the electorate he had performed notably in some areas, and with less distinction in others, largely foreign.

He had, in the early days of 1964, carried out the legislative program of the late John Kennedy probably better than the assassinated President could have done himself, going on, then, to win his own election by the greatest majority in the nation's history. He had moved, in 1965, from the New Frontier to the Great Society in a search to eliminate, or at least mitigate, hunger, ignorance and the suppression of human rights, not only in this country but throughout the world. He had tried, if unsuccessfully, to move the Vietnam war from the battlefield to the conference table.

And in the early days of 1966 just past, he had sent a State of the Union Message to Congress, askings funds to continue and expand the Great Society program, despite the rising costs of national defense, most particularly the war in Vietnam. He followed it twelve days later with a budget request for appropriations of $112.8 billion for the fiscal year 1966-67, to pay for his programs.

The conflict in Vietnam, he told Congress, was not an isolated episode, but "another great event in the policy that we have followed with strong consistency since World War II.

"The touchstone of that policy," he continued, "is the interest of the United States—the welfare and freedom of the people of the United States. But nations sink when they see that interest only through a narrow glass.

"In a world that has grown small and dangerous, pursuit of narrow aims could bring decay and even disaster.

"An America that is mighty beyond description—yet living in a hostile or despairing world—would be neither safe, nor free to build a civilization to liberate the spirit of man.

"In this pursuit we helped rebuild Western Europe. We gave our aid to Greece and Turkey, and we defended the freedom of Berlin.

"In this pursuit we have defended again Communist aggression—in Korea under President Truman—in the Formosa Straits under President Eisenhower—in Cuba under President Kennedy—and again in Vietnam."

But, said the President, we will not permit those who fire upon us in Vietnam to win a victory over the desires and the intentions of all the American people.

"This nation," he continued, "is mighty enough, its society is healthy enough, its people are strong enough, to pursue our goals in the rest of the world while still building a Great Society here at home."

He then asked that Congress help him continue the programs for health and education, the war on poverty, the foreign aid attack on hunger, disease and ignorance, slum clearance, air and water pollution, crime and civil rights.

"I have not come here to ask for pleasant luxuries or idle pleasures," he told Congress. "I have come here to recommend that you, the representatives of the richest nation on earth, you, the elected servants of a people who live in abundance unmatched on this globe, you bring the most urgent decencies of life to all of your fellow Americans."

Admittedly, there would be penalties to pay; not in actual increased taxes, but in the deferral of certain excise tax reductions authorized in 1965, and by the acceleration of corporate and personal income tax collections, and Social Security payments. These measures, the President said, would yield $1.2 billion in Fiscal 1965-66 and $4.8 billion in Fiscal 1966-67. Additional funds to cover the increase in the 1966-67 budget would be met by increased receipts from a stronger national economy. He told the Congress:

"The unprecedented and uninterrupted economic growth of the past five years has clearly demonstrated the contribution that appropriate fiscal action can make to national prosperity. In calendar year 1966, the nation's output of goods and services—the gross national product—is expected to grow by $46 billion over 1965, reaching $722 billion, plus or minus $5 billion. This increase will follow on the heels of last year's growth, when the real gross national product advanced by 5½ per cent. During that year:

"Nearly 2½ million additional jobs were created; countless new and previously idle plants and machines were thrown into productive use; consumer and business incomes reached record levels; the unemployment rate fell to 4.1 per cent, the lowest in more than eight years.

It was the third budget and the third legislative program Lyndon Johnson had presented to Congress. The first had been in January, 1964, when he had asked a joint session to enact the programs of John Kennedy, "not because of our sorrow or sympathy, but because they are right."

Johnson's handling of the legislative program demonstrated then, for any who may have forgotten his days as Senate Majority Leader, his consummate mastery of the art of maneuvering on Capitol Hill. Late in 1963, after Johnson had picked up the reins of the Presidency in November, the measures most imperatively wanted by the White House were tightly locked in various committees of the House and Senate. The tax cut bill, passed by the House, could not be budged out of the Senate Finance Committee. The Civil Rights bill was being held up in the House Rules Committee. Other measures were stalled in other parts of the legislative machinery.

The proposed tax cut, applied to a government that was already operating on deficit spending—borrowed money— was a radical thought. The theory behind it, of course, was that the tax reduction would so stimulate production, by making more money available for such things as plant expansion, that the increase in the gross national product would produce more than enough taxes to offset the reduction.

The bill passed, was signed into law and its enactment broke the log jam in Congress.

Johnson moved from tax matters to the Civil Rights bill, the most bitterly controversial of the Kennedy program. The threat of a discharge petition moved it out of the House Rules Committee and in the Senate the seldom-invoked Rule of Cloture checked a filibuster, both of which moves had been Johnson-inspired. The measure passed and was signed into law on July 2, 1964.

Other Kennedy measures had fairly clear sailing: the Wilderness Bill set aside 9,200,000 acres of national forest lands to remain just what they are—wilderness areas, unspoiled by man's commercial exploitation, with another 19,700,000 saved for possible future inclusion; the Mass Transit Act, authorizing $375,000,000 for bus and rail systems in congested urban areas: the $1 billion Highway Aid bill; and the earmarking of another $1 billion for research into the major crippling illnesses of the nation.

And, on August 2, President Johnson signed the one major measure passed by the 88th Congress which was peculiarly his own, the Economic Opportunity Act, a $947,500 million bill directed toward the fight against poverty.

The year 1965, Lyndon Johnson's first as the elected President in his own right, became also the year of the Great Society. His concept of the Great Society was first offered to the American people, and to such of the world as might care, on May 22, 1964, in a speech to the graduating class of the University of Michigan at Ann Arbor. It subsequently replaced the Kennedy New Frontier as the creed and doctrine of the Johnson Administration. The President said:

"The Great Society rests on abundance and liberty for all. It demands an end to poverty and racial injustice, to which we are totally committed in our time. But that is just the beginning. The Great Society is a place where every child can find knowledge to enrich his mind and to enlarge his talents. It is a place where the city of man serves not only the needs of the body and the demands of commerce, but the desire for beauty and hunger for community.

"It is a place where man can renew contact with nature. It is a place which honors creation for its own sake and for what it adds to the understanding of the race. It is a place where men are more concerned with the quality of their goals than the quantity of their goods. But most of all, the Great Society is not a safe harbor, a resting place, a final objective, a finished work. It is a challenge constantly renewed, beckoning us toward a destiny where the meaning of our lives matches the marvelous products of our labor."

President Johnson's concept of the Great Society * is one not only affluent but one which can control its own economic growth, and one which can be governed by consensus.

While the Great Society envisions a collection of expanding and desirable programs, from education to urban development, it also is conditioned upon governmental ability to regulate national productivity to the point where the age-old predicament of a population of "haves and have-nots" will be eliminated. The costs of such programs as slum eradication and the abolishment of poverty can be covered by controlled increase of the nation's output of wealth. This controverts the normal, to many, assumption that the division of the national loaf is fixed, and that if some take more, others must take less.

The word "consensus," by Johnson's definition, means simply that, to achieve the goals of the Great Society, the programs, both individual and as a whole, must have the overwhelming support of the American people. Consensus

* The term "Great Society" was the title of a book published in 1914 by Graham Wallas, an Englishman, who was an original member of the Fabian Society. In his book, Wallas proposed that the lives of everybody be organized toward the goal that they would, as a collective norm, think, act (and enjoy) together under a visionary and elite supervisory class.

to the President means not a simple majority, but more like the sixty-five per cent-plus by which he was elected in November, 1964.

His State of the Union Message, delivered in terms of the Great Society, called for: a massive education program to aid schools of all religions; medical care for the aged; new programs to rescue the cities from blight, to increase the beauty of the countryside and to end the "poisoning of the rivers and the air we breathe"; a redoubling of the war against poverty; the enforcement of the civil rights law and the elimination of barriers to the right to vote; better transportation systems, an extension of the minimum wage law to uncovered persons.

If, as many political observers thought, Lyndon Johnson's success with the 88th Congress in 1964 was notable, his achievements with the 89th in 1965 were virtually phenomenal.

The President's domestic proposals were aimed largely at improving the Great Society concepts and here Congress granted virtually his every request. Of major importance were: $1 billion for aid to elementary and secondary students, plus some thirty other educational measures; some thirty-five health measures, including medicare for the aged, financed under the Social Security program; increased Social Security benefits; a $1.5 billion anti-poverty program and a dozen other welfare bills; the establishment of a Cabinet-level Department of Housing and Urban Development (to which he named Robert Weaver, the nation's first Negro Cabinet member).

In the field of Foreign Policy, Johnson asked for and obtained a long-sought immigration reform measure which replaced the old and out-moded national origins quota system with one based on preferential admission, largely determined by the skills of the prospective immigrant. His foreign aid requests were cut only slightly on their way through Congress and three separate pleas for funds for defense of Vietnam were granted in full.

As measure after measure came back from Capitol Hill for the President's signature, one Washington political writer was moved to write, in some wonder:

"Congress has obviously accepted the assumption that Papa knows best."

Despite the scope and volume of Johnson victories, however, there were also defeats, with most of them scheduled for another round in 1966. The most significant came in the field of labor legislation, when Congress refused to go along with repeal of the Right-to-Work provisions of the Taft-Hartley Act and with the increase of the minimum wage and its extension of coverage. Another notable defeat came in legislation to provide home rule for the District of Columbia. The Senate passed an Administration-sponsored measure which was stalled in the House Rules Committee and brought to the floor by discharge petition only after great persuasion by the White House. Then, in a bit of procedural legerdemain, the House found itself voting for a substitute bill. It passed, but was so different in content and intent from the Senate measure there was little hope of compromising the two. The Congress also failed to vote funds for the rent supplement program, designed to aid low-income families which could not obtain standard housing within their own incomes.

President Johnson could, in the Spring of 1966, look back with considerable satisfaction at the progress of his Great Society programs. They were programs he understood with the full clarity of first-hand experience and certainly they were uppermost in his mind. Lyndon Johnson needs no one to explain poverty to him; he grew up in poverty. It is doubtful that before the age of fifteen he ever stepped inside a house, let alone lived in one, which had an indoor toilet or hot running water. His own formal education, by today's standards, was shabby, and he narrowly missed being a school dropout.

His anti-poverty program, under the more formal name of the Economic Opportunity Program, is, said President Johnson, "a program to help people help themselves." It comprises some ten major sub programs which cost $1.2 billion in 1965-66, with $1.6 billion programmed for 1966-67.

More than a million children and youths were expected to receive help from Head Start, Remedial Education, Neighborhood Youth Corps and Job Corps in 1966. Nine hundred Community Action Programs to fight poverty were being set in motion, along with programs to provide work experience and adult literacy training. Other poverty projects were:

> Job Corps: 25 urban training centers and 99 rural centers with a total capacity for 39,000 young men and 6,000 young women.
> Work and Training Programs: work, training, basic education and related services for 400,000 youths and adults.
> Plus: training for 400,000 migrant workers; basic education for 75,000 adults; small business loans for 15,500 low-income rural families.

All in all, including Social Security, medical benefits and public welfare, the Johnson Administration expected to spend in Fiscal 1966-67 some $21 billion, $4 billion more than during the previous year, on some form of aid to the nation's 34 million people who live in poverty.

In the field of education, the major victories for Johnson in his first elected year were aid to elementary and secondary education, with emphasis on helping individual needy children, and the college aid programs of scholarships to college students. The President budgeted $2.8 billion for 1966-67 Federal aid to education, an increase of 23 per cent over 1965-66.

In addition to his new cabinet-level Department of Housing and Urban Development (HUD), President Johnson pushed forward several housing programs in 1965-66 and projected them into the next year: public housing and housing for the aged, urban renewal (and beautification), and new federal aid for land development. The public housing programs, estimated to increase from $249 million in 1966 to $261 million in 1967, were largely in low-rent public housing. Urban renewal expenditures, nearing the half billion mark in 1967, carried an emphasis on renewal without wholesale clearance of large areas, as had sometimes happened in the past.

As an addition to the Kennedy Civil Rights bill which Johnson had pushed through Congress in 1964, he added in 1965 a measure to eliminate barriers to Negro voting. The bill suspended all literacy test requirements and allowed appointment of federal examiners for enforcement.

The number of health and welfare programs passed in 1965 by the 89th Congress totalled fifty. The two which would probably be deemed most important and far-reaching were both tied in with Social Security: a hospital insurance program for the aged, financed under Social Security, and a seven per cent increase in Social Security benefits. Others included a program to disseminate information on and provide for diagnosis and treatment of heart disease, as well as for cancer and stroke patients, grants for community health centers and the construction of facilities for health research.

In his 1966 State of the Union Message, President Johnson told Congress: "I recommend that you attack the wasteful and degrading poisoning of our rivers and, as the cornerstone of this effort, clean completely entire large river basins." He followed this up with a budget request for 1966-67 of $331 million, to be used in the campaign against both air and water pollution, largely by the Water Pollution Control Administration, recently established.

During 1965, President Johnson had enunciated natural beauty enhancement as a part of the Great Society. Of the twelve park areas across the country he requested, Congress gave him four, adding programs of federal aid, aimed at hopefully controlling billboards and junkyards along highways.

Paradoxically, and despite his imaginative and forceful programs to raise the standards of living of the American people—already the highest in the world—and his assaults on poverty, ignorance and misery, according to national polls, the President's popularity in the Spring of 1966 stood at its lowest point since he took office in November, 1963.

The reason was, of course, the war in Vietnam, a war which might be stoutly defended, but which no American really wanted, and probably no one less than Lyndon Johnson. At this point, the hopes of his great Peace Offensive were fading and the nation debated the course of action of the least popular war in the nation's history.

Since 1954 and the Geneva Accord, under which the French withdrew from Vietnam and the divided country agreed to an uneasy peace under the observance of an International Commission, succeeding American Administrations have participated in keeping that peace with varying degrees of reluctance.

The United States took part in the Geneva Agreement only as an observer and did not sign the accord, but did assume responsibility for the protection of the Republic of South Vietnam, since the French were pulling out.

Each successive President—Eisenhower, Kennedy and Johnson—and his advisors have recognized the danger of a "falling domino" reaction in Southeast Asia if the North Vietnam Communists (backed by the Red Chinese) are permitted to take over the whole of Vietnam; that is, that the neighboring nations of Laos, Cambodia, Thailand, Burma, the Malayan Peninsula—and even the Philippines—would be subjected to succeeding and perhaps irresistible Communist pressure.

After the Geneva Accord in 1954, the truce between the divided segments of the nation held until 1959, when the Communists in the North began their "War of National Liberation," a distorted term both Red China and Russia use to cloak guerilla aggression, either open or disguised.

The aggression began with classic guerilla methods of banditry, vandalism and selective terror; in fact, there is considerable evidence that the North Vietnamese simply reactivated the old guerilla units which had operated so effectively against the French, with the same leaders, the same methods and the same floating or underground bases of operation.

The Vietnam situation smouldered quietly, if dangerously, during the early part of Johnson's first year in office, although, after a conference with United States officials in Honolulu in June, 1964, on the whole Asian situation, he issued a warning:

"There can be little doubt in the minds of the Communists," he said, "that we are prepared to help the Vietnamese repel Communist aggression. Our support of Thailand is equally clear." On July 22, during a visit of Prince Abdul Rahman, Prime Minister of Malaysia, he pledged support of that nation also.

The real beginning of open warfare came after August 2, 1964, when the Defense Department announced that three North Vietnamese PT (for Patrol Torpedo) boats had earlier that day attacked the United States destroyer *Maddox* while it was on patrol in the Gulf of Tonkin, in international waters some thirty miles off the coast of North Vietnam. Another attack followed on August 4. In both, the destroyer targets, undamaged themselves, returned the fire, sinking or damaging five attacking craft.

Johnson's reaction, after a meeting with the National Security Council and both Democratic and Republican Congressmen, was made clear over a nation-wide television address, shortly before midnight that same day. He reviewed the Gulf of Tonkin incident, stressed that up until that time our action in Vietnam had been defensive and continued:

"Repeated acts of violence against the armed forces of the United States must be met not only with alert defense but with positive reply. That reply is being given as I speak to you tonight. Air action is now in execution against gunboats and certain supporting facilities in North Vietnam . . . used in these hostile operations." (It was eight hours earlier in Vietnam, that is, about four in the afternoon.) The next day, August 5, Secretary of Defense Robert Mc-Namara said that the air mission referred to had bombed North Vietnamese naval craft, their bases and an oil storage depot. Twenty-five PT boats had been destroyed or damaged and the oil depot ninety per cent destroyed, he reported. Two American planes were shot down and two others damaged.

Speaking at Syracuse University that night, the President again reviewed the Tonkin situation and said:

"President Eisenhower sought—and President Kennedy sought—the same objectives that I still seek:

"That the Governments of Southeast Asia honor the international agreements which apply in the area. That those governments leave each other alone; that they resolve their differences peacefully; that they devote their talents to bettering the lives of their peoples by working against poverty and disease and ignorance."

Early in 1965, the war in Vietnam was escalated another step when, in retaliation for guerilla attacks and bombings directed against American military personnel in barracks and hotel billets (as opposed to actual combat activities) the President ordered and began carrying out bombing attacks against supply dumps and guerilla staging areas in Vietnam. And, as the Summer of 1965 advanced, American infantry, paratroop, aerial cavalry and marine divisions went into ground action in increasing strength.

By the Spring of 1966 the forces in Vietnam were estimated at:

Vietcong guerillas, 100,000. (The word "Vietcong" means Red Viet.")

Vietcong political infiltrators, 40,000.

Vietcong regulars, including 7 to 9 regiments of North Vietnamese regulars, 80,000.

South Vietnamese troops, 679,000, including a small Air Force and Navy.

United States Ground and Air Forces, 197,000.

United States Naval Task Force, 50,000.

Australian, New Zealand and South Korean Forces, 20,000.

The Vietcong was judged to control twenty-five per cent of South Vietnam, but this did not include any large towns or cities. They collected taxes from much of the area, although it might be called tribute, and in some places even delivered mail.

President Johnson's Peace Offensive began in early December, 1965, in conjunction with two Christmas and New Year truces, which the Vietcong violated liberally. The President suspended North Vietnam bombing operations and sent a dozen of his top diplomatic officials to twice that many countries (including Averell Harriman, Ambassador at Large to Russia and other Iron Curtain nations), presumably to explain the American position and stress the American desire to move the Vietnam situation from the jungle battlefields to the conference table.

When Vietnam's President Ho Chi Minh replied only with accusations of deceit, war mongering and aggression, and made a renewal of his demands that the Vietcong be recognized as the sole government of South Vietnam, President Johnson ordered bombing renewed. He coupled this action with an urgent appeal to the United Nations to use every influence and pressure at its command to bring about peace.

Other foreign situations and incidents brought further

problems to the President.

The first came early in January of 1964, when clashes between American and Panamanian students over the flying of the two flags culminated in rioting which left twenty-five dead and some 350 persons injured. Panamanian President Robert Chiari severed diplomatic relations with the United States and protested to the United Nations.

In typical Johnson fashion, the President picked up the telephone and called Chiari for a conference in which both agreed on measures to stop further disorders.

On February 22, President Johnson flew to the West Coast, where he spoke at the University of California, in Los Angeles, along with President Adolfo Lopez Mateos of Mexico. Johnson's speech included these words:

"We seek a growing partnership with all our friends and we will never retreat from our obligations to any ally. Nor will we ever be intimidated by any state anywhere at any time in the world that chooses to make itself our adversary."

Later, the two Presidents paid a call upon a third—former President Dwight Eisenhower—at nearby Palm Desert.

Earlier that month, Cuba's Fidel Castro had threatened to cut off the water supply to the US Naval base at Guantanamo until thirty-eight Cuban fishermen detained by the US Coast Guard were released. Johnson retorted that the fishermen had been within a mile and a half of American shores, and thus were violating American waters. He sent a Rear Admiral to cut the water main (instead of fighting to keep it open) and had an emergency supply plant put into effect. The next day, he ordered the Defense Department to discharge some 2,500 Cuban employees of the base (unless they chose to live there and spend their wages there) and to start construction of a salt water conversion plant on the base. Meantime, the American personnel there were supplied by tanker. The fishermen were later released with suspended sentences. The water conversion plant is now completed and operating effectively.

The year 1964 also saw several visits from foreign potentates. (Johnson had announced that he would not leave the country until a Vice President could be elected.) King Hussein of Jordan arrived and spent April 14-15 in Washington, conferring with President Johnson over Arab-Israeli differences. In a speech at the National Press Club, Hussein said Israel was a "trouble maker" and suggested that the United States should take a new look at its Palestine policy. In a statement after the meeting of the two heads of state, President Johnson pledged the United States to continue aiding Jordan to "attain a viable and self-sustaining economy." The Premier of Israel, Levi Eshkol, followed Hussein to Washington in June. At the conclusion of their talks, President Johnson reaffirmed "support for the territorial integrity and political independence of all countries in the Middle East" and also reaffirmed United States opposition to aggression.

West German Chancellor Ludwig Erhard also arrived in the United States during that same June. President Johnson pledged all reasonable help in bringing about the unification of Germany. Chancellor Erhard promised no serious trading with Communist China.

There were deaths, too, among the notable, both foreign and domestic. On April 5, the President attended the funeral of that great old warrior General Douglas MacArthur, who had, twenty-two years earlier in Australia, decorated the

President with the Silver Star for gallantry under fire. As described earlier in this book, Johnson, who served briefly as a Naval Lieutenant Commander in the early days of World War II, was there on an inspection trip for President Roosevelt and narrowly missed being shot down off New Guinea while he was flying as an observer in a bomber. In May, 1964, the President sent Secretary of State Dean Rusk to represent him at the funeral and cremation ceremonies for Jawaharlal Nehru, Prime Minister of India. He ordered a thirty-day period of mourning for the nation when former President Herbert Hoover died on October 30 of the same year.

Probably the two most momentous events of his first year came in October, 1964, within the space of twenty-four hours. Nikita Khrushchev was stripped of all powers by his comrades on the Communist Party's Central Committee, and summarily ousted as party secretary and premier; and Premier Mao Tse-tung announced from Peiping that China had exploded a nuclear bomb.

The year 1965 brought visits to President Johnson from Japanese Premier Eisaker Sato (in January) for a discussion of the Communist situation; and from Italian Premier Aldo Moro (in April) for talks on Vietnam and NATO. It also brought deaths.

Adlai Stevenson, the United States representative to the United Nations, died on July 14, and President Johnson led the mourners at a state funeral in the National Cathedral. Later he named Supreme Court Justice Arthur Goldberg to replace Stevenson at the UN. When Sir Winston Churchill died in England (earlier, in January), the President did not attend the funeral, but sent representatives. Former President Eisenhower attended unofficially, by special invitation.

Among the events of the year for President Johnson, two were of major importance, one in the foreign field, the other extremely personal. The first was a revolution in the Dominican Republic, the second was a major operation for the removal of the Presidential gall bladder.

On April 24-25, 1965, a coup by military leaders overthrew the government of the Dominican Republic, a triumvirate headed by Donald Reid Cabral. The intention of the military men, they said, was to restore to power exiled former President Juan Bosch. The result, however, was an armed forces power struggle between Bosch and anti-Bosch forces.

President Johnson moved swiftly in ordering the Navy to evacuate 1,172 United States civilians on the island, and then the next day, April 28, he ordered a force of 400 marines to Santo Domingo, the capital, to protect the lives of Americans who had remained there, and of other foreign nationals.

The marine units were followed shortly by 4,200 airborne troops. Then, on May 2, President Johnson announced that Communist activists had taken over the uprising. Speaking over a national television network, he said:

"Communist leaders, many of them trained in Cuba, seeing a chance to increase disorder and to gain a foothold, joined the revolution. What began as a popular democratic revolution that was committed to democracy and social justice moved into the hands of a band of Communist conspirators. . . . The American nations cannot, must not and will not permit the establishment of another Communist government in the Western Hemisphere." Johnson later named and identified many of the Communist leaders on the island, although the importance and effectiveness of a number were disputed by other political sources.

On May 5, by which time the United States had committed 12,430 Army and 6,925 Marine troops into the revolt area, the Organization of the American States succeeded in negotiating a truce, later setting up a peace-keeping force of 8,000 men. Both actions came after United States motions made to the OAS.

By the Spring of 1966, with the truce broken and patched up several times, a provisional president of the Dominican Republic was in power and many of the rebel leaders had been "exiled" to diplomatic posts abroad.

The President's own personal crisis came on October 8, 1965, when, after carefully preparing the nation with spaced announcements, he went to Bethesda Naval Hospital, where doctors removed a "poorly functioning" gall bladder and a kidney stone from his right ureter.

It was a major operation and a serious one, but not one the doctors considered critically dangerous, they said beforehand. Their prognosis proved correct. Five hours after the surgery, Johnson climbed from his bed and took a few steps. The next day he signed a few minor bills and talked with White House aides. On October 10, he held a short press conference and talked with Vice President Hubert Humphrey, who had stood by during the critical period, but who was never called upon to make decisions on behalf of the President.

On October 21, Johnson visited other Naval hospital patients—marines who had been wounded in the Dominican

Republic affair (eight American military had been killed and forty-nine wounded)—and then returned to the White House. Two days later, he flew to the LBJ ranch in Johnson City, where his convalescence was completed.

11

☆

The Election of Lyndon Johnson

Lyndon Baines Johnson was elected President of the United States on November 3, 1964, by the greatest popular vote plurality of any Presidential election in American history.

His Republican opponent, Senator Barry Goldwater, had hoped to mobilize a massive army of conservatives that would overwhelm the Democratic party. Instead, he aroused the Democrats, independents and moderate Republicans into a coalition which buried him and his supporters under a tidal wave of votes. The actual figures were: Johnson 43,126,506 and Goldwater 27,176,799.

Barry Goldwater, born January 1, 1909, is a native of Arizona and a graduate of the state's university. He served in the Army Air Corps during World War II, rising to the rank of major general in the reserves after the war. He was elected to his Senate seat in 1952, campaigning on a conservative platform and continuing as a conservative in the Senate. He was elected chairman of the Republican Campaign Committee in 1956, a position which served as an organizational stepping stone to his nomination by the Republican party.

Hubert Humphrey, Lyndon Johnson's teammate on the Democratic ticket, exploded into political prominence in the late 1940s as an articulate, liberal boy-wonder from the Middle West. He managed Minnesota's Democratic State campaign in 1944, was elected Mayor of Minneapolis in 1945 and 1947, and then to the United States Senate in 1948. At the 1948 Democratic Convention, he led a convention fight over Civil Rights which forced the Southern delegations to walk out and form their own party, the Dixiecrats.

As Minority Leader, and later Majority Leader, Lyndon Johnson recognized the new Senator as a potentially useful and valuable part of the Senate establishment. He helped Humphrey mend his fences with his Southern colleagues and coached him in the tactics of Senate maneuvering— the attack, the retreat, the trade and the compromise. He also taught him the difference between that which can be done and that which should be done, but cannot be done.

Humphrey was born on May 27, 1911, in Wallace, South Dakota. He holds a degree in Pharmacy from Denver College, a Bachelor's degree in political science from the University of Minnesota and a Master's degree in political science from the University of Louisiana. The military turned him down for World War II for physical reasons (a hernia). He is married and has four children.

Humphrey announced for the Vice Presidency in 1956 and the Presidency in 1960, failing on both occasions. When Lyndon Johnson was nominated to run with John Kennedy in 1960, Humphrey became Majority Whip, the second ranking Senate Democratic leadership post. His voting record is as liberal as that of anyone in Congress and the legislation he advocated was imaginative and ahead of the times —the Test Ban Treaty, Peace Corps, Job Corps, Medicare, all of which he proposed long before they were seriously considered by Congress. In 1964, he floor-managed the Civil Rights bill through the long, arduous filibuster.

Senator Goldwater announced formally that he was seeking the Republican Presidential nomination on January 3, 1964, at Paradise City, Arizona. In his announcement speech, he said:

"I have decided to do this . . . because I have not heard from any Republican candidate a declaration of conscience or political position that could possibly offer to the American people a clear choice in the next Presidential election.

"One of the great attributes of our American two-party system has always been the reflected differences in principle. As a general rule, one party has emphasized individual liberty and the other has favored the extension of government power. I am convinced that today a majority in the Republican party believes in the essential emphasis on individual liberty." The phrasing of his opening announcement became the basic theme of his campaign.

Senator Goldwater's rivals for the Republican nomination were Governor Nelson Rockefeller of New York, Governor William Scranton of Pennsylvania and Governor George Romney of Michigan. All three were moderate Republicans, as were Richard Nixon, defeated by a close margin in a race for the Presidency by John Kennedy in 1960 and still hopeful, Ambassador (to Vietnam) Cabot Lodge, who never announced, and Senator Margaret Chase Smith of Maine, the first woman candidate to seriously announce for the Presidency.

In the States where nomination is by primary, where the voters are permitted a choice of candidates, Goldwater did not fare well, except in the last and biggest—California. In a surprising show of popular strength there, he defeated Rockefeller, thereby virtually knocking the New Yorker out of the race. At the Republican National Convention Goldwater was nominated on the first ballot and he named Representative William Edward Miller of New York as his running mate. The platform adopted was a reflection of the views of the Goldwater faction. It called for a larger military establishment, balanced budget, tax reduction and the end of fighting in Vietnam.

Since Lyndon Johnson was the lone candidate under serious consideration, the only suspense at the Democratic National Convention in Atlantic City, New Jersey, August 23-26, centered around who would be the Vice Presidential candidate.

Late in July, President Johnson clarified his own position in the matter of running mates succinctly. He issued an announcement which said:

"I have reached the conclusion that it would be inadvisable for me to recommend to the convention any member of my Cabinet or any of those who meet regularly with the Cabinet. In this regard, because their names have been mentioned in the press, I have personally informed the Secretary of State, Mr. Rusk, the Secretary of Defense, Mr. McNamara, the Attorney General, Mr. Kennedy, and the Secretary of Agriculture, Mr. Freeman, of my decision. I have communicated this to the United States Ambassador to the United Nations, Mr. Stevenson, and the head of the Peace Corps, Mr. Shriver. In this manner the list has been narrowed. I shall continue to give the most thoughtful consideration to the choice of the man whom I will recommend and I shall make my decision known in due course."

This narrowed the list down actually to two or three people. These were Senators Eugene McCarthy and Humphrey, both of Minnesota, and Senator Thomas Dodd of Connecticut. (McCarthy had certain advantages: in addition to being able and respected, he was a Roman Catholic—to balance the Republican's Miller—and while a liberal, he was not so surely identified with Civil Rights as was Humphrey. Dodd was considered as an outside possibility.)

Lyndon Johnson contrived to wring the last bit of suspense from his selection, delaying any announcement until he was leaving Washington on August 24, on his way to the convention, where he had just been nominated by acclamation. He then told the country he had decided that Humphrey "would be the best equipped man in this nation to be President if something happened to the President." Humphrey was also nominated by acclamation. The Democratic platform advocated combining military power with efforts to end the arms race, economy in government, expanded social programs and conservation of natural resources, including great tracts of wilderness lands—and, of course, Civil Rights and the elimination of social and economic causes which create lawlessness.

The earlier sparring and the conventions were only the preliminaries for the intense campaign of the last two months before election.

The Johnson campaign, when it got started, on Labor Day, Monday, September 7, in Detroit, Michigan, was one of sheer exuberance and reminiscent of Texas. The whole family joined in the activities.

In one of a series of luncheons, Johnson sent telegrams

inviting 260 top American businessmen to lunch at the White House. Washington National Airport had to utilize an unused runway to park some ninety company aircraft. Secretaries McNamara and Rusk, and later the President, addressed the industrialists, explaining Administration policy.

In one campaign swing alone, the President made twenty-four unscheduled stops where he left the official train to mingle with the crowds. While walking the family beagles around the White House grounds, he and Mrs. Johnson opened the gates to let the crowds of sight-seers in, to shake hands and chat.

Mrs. Johnson organized the Lady Bird Special through the South to conduct a whistle-stop tour. She rode at the end of the train in an old observation car which had been brightly painted and was decorated with scalloped red and white awnings. Rolling through Virginia, North Carolina and South Carolina, she drew large sympathetic crowds. Her trip was so successful and she was having such an obvious good time that her husband twice joined her train (by plane) to share the fun. Both of the Johnson girls, Lynda Bird and Luci Baines, were constantly with their parents—or on their own—participating in the campaign. It was made unmistakably clear that the members of the Johnson family, all four of them, are not only effective campaigners but they enjoy doing it.

There is nothing more American and nothing more traditionally splendid in America than that quadrennial pageant—the Presidential Inauguration. It is a time of national rebirth; a newly-elected President takes the solemn oath of office. It is also a time of parade and pageantry, of parties and balls, of laughter and victory celebration.

The 1965 Inaugural had an exaggerated air of Texas. While on the campaign trail, Lyndon Johnson had said "Y'all come" and they came, from the banks of the Pedernales to the banks of the Pecos, an estimated 3,000 strong. The ten-gallon hat and the Southern drawl blended with the rich furs and clipped Bostonian accents.

The swearing-in ceremonies at the Capitol, the parade to the White House and the great Presidential ball were on Wednesday, January 20, but the major celebration began the night before with a reception at the White House honoring the new Vice President.

Ten thousand people attended and within an hour after six, when the doors were opened to the two ballrooms and large foyer needed to accommodate the crowd, all three areas were dense with women in bright evening dresses and men in dinner jackets. The bars and the hors d'oeuvre tables were barely accessible. Vice President Humphrey arrived via the kitchen, the only way he could get in through the throngs. Between breaks in the cheering, he introduced his family, including wife, children, sister, brothers, in-laws and cousins. Introductions for the Minnesota political family followed—Senator Eugene McCarthy, Secretary of Agriculture, Orville Freeman, and Governor Karl Rolvaag. A good share of the crowd was made up of Minnesotans, but there were also diplomats from other nations—South America, Europe and the Iron Curtain countries—and just loyal Democrats with $10, the price of admission.

A dance, sponsored by the Young Democrats, followed the reception and it was equally gay and informal. There was no such thing as a stranger in the house. The dance was so heavily subscribed that two locations were needed. Lynda appeared at one dance and Luci attended the second. The

President attended a special Inaugural concert and then other private parties.

Inaugural Day, Wednesday, January 20, began at 2 A.M. for the first elaborate floats as they began staging for the procession from the Capitol to the White House. The parade started moving at one-thirty in the afternoon, and ended just before dark, at five.

President Johnson left the White House shortly before noon and rode to the Capitol.

There, hatless and dark-suited, without an overcoat, he placed his hand on the family Bible held by Lady Bird Johnson and took, from Chief Justice Earl Warren, the thirty-five-word oath of office which signified, in this case, not a transfer of power but a continuing of power. Following the Inaugural address and its promise of personal dedication of achievement of the Great Society in America, the President and the First Lady lunched at the Capitol with long-time congressional friends, according to tradition.

After lunch President and Mrs. Johnson stepped into their car to lead the parade. It had barely started when he spotted the band from the Southwest State College at San Marcos, Texas, his alma mater. Each state was allowed one float and one band in the parade, save Texas and Minnesota, which were permitted two bands each, and one of the pair from the Southwest State led all the rest. Seeing the band ready to march, the President stopped his car, climbed out and went over to shake hands with a hundred startled, if pleased, girls and boys.

The parade itself was in line with the high aims of the Great Society. Discouraged from local hoopla, the states were encouraged to feature (and did) such topics as the War on Poverty, Food for Peace, Urban Renewal and Preservation of the Wilderness. Except for marching units of the Services, there was no military participation. An Air Force flyover was cancelled.

The Inaugural ball was held in five different locations— at the huge armory and in the city's four largest hotel ballrooms. It was like the Vice Presidential reception, only on a grander scale. All of the rooms were crowded, but that was part of the show and no one cared. President Johnson and Vice President Humphrey, with their wives and some of their children, at least, made every ball, and spoke at each one.

At one point the President looked out over the throng and said:

"Whatever else you may say about the Great Society, it sure is crowded."

At each ball, the President danced with the First Lady, with Mrs. Humphrey, usually with one of his daughters and occasionally with a thrilled feminine visitor. The Inauguration ended for him well past midnight, when he returned to the White House with Mrs. Johnson.

Once home, he had to read from his briefing notes what had happened in the outside world that day. He must think again of the affairs of the nation, since he was beginning four years of service as the duly elected President of the United States.

12

☆

Return to Johnson City

On January 20, 1969, Richard Nixon was inaugurated President of the United States, and that night he was a drop-in guest of half a dozen inaugural balls held in the armory and in Washington hotels.

Lyndon Johnson, having escorted his successor to the Capitol for the swearing-in ceremony, chose that night to make his farewells to Washington, which had been his home as clerk, Representative, Senator, Vice President and President for thirty-eight years.

And as he waited at Andrews Air Force Base early in the evening for the jet which would carry him and his family to Austin, where he would shift to a smaller craft for the flight to the LBJ Ranch at Johnson City, Lyndon Johnson had a last small triumph, and possibly a quiet laugh.

For crowded at the ramp on the chilly January night were probably more people than any one of the inaugural balls could boast. They were there for a last demonstration of affection for Lyndon Johnson and they heard him return their good-byes with laughter which was close to tears. The plane he boarded was the same Air Force One which had brought him from Dallas on November 23, 1963, newly sworn-in as President.

A few nights earlier he had ridden from the White House down Independence Avenue and the Mall to Capitol Hill, where he made a last appearance before a joint session of Congress to deliver a farewell message in person.

In the days preceding, as he worked over drafts of the speech he would deliver, Johnson wavered frequently on his decision to go in person. No President had done so since John Adams in 1801. The President was greatly conscious of the unpopularity of the Vietnam war and the transmittal of that unpopularity to him personally; he knew that many people actually considered him a dishonest and dishonorable man. From these things had come his decision not to run in 1968.

But once made, he could not have regretted the decision to appear personally. In the great hall of the House, where as a handsome, black-haired youth thirty-eight years before he had picked up extra money serving as doorkeeper (his regular job was secretary to Congressman Kleberg), Lyndon Johnson was greeted by a standing, cheering ovation that went on in waves for five minutes.

Looking up to the gallery, Mr. Johnson could see his wife, her eyes glistening, his daughters and his grandson, Lyndon Nugent. No respector of persons, young Lyn grew restless shortly after the speech was begun, and had to be taken out.

The farewell message was nonpartisan, with praise for leaders and the rank and file on both sides of the aisle. He spoke of the achievements of his administration, of medicare, headstart, the model cities, the decrease in joblessness, of civil rights and college scholarships, a more stable monetary system, and with regret that peace in Vietnam had not been accomplished. He was interrupted 51 times with applause.

Then, Lyndon Johnson went back to Texas where he is really more at home than anywhere else in the world. The weather has been good there since his return, the winters sunny and the rains coming at the right time. People there say "Lyndon orders the weather."

In his sixties now, Mr. Johnson's hair is completely white, and his eyes echo the tiredness of the lines of his face. Even the herculean energy has lessened; the man from Johnson City is often content to relax and take things easy.

He spends much of the time outdoors, driving the big Lincoln, riding the big horses that fit his own large frame, ranging the pastures among the Herefords and the deer, which like other crops are harvested every fall for steaks and the venison sausage which has always been the former President's favorite breakfast fare, before, during, and after the Washington days.

Mr. Johnson likes his old friends and likes to be with them; usually he is with one or more during the course of any one day, but sometimes he rides alone, or as alone as one can be with the Secret Service guards who are never too far away.

The transition from President of the United States to private citizen cannot be an easy one. There are things to miss; the awesome power, the pomp, the obsequious attention to every word.

"I want to miss them," said Lyndon Johnson. "It hurts good." The "hurting good" can be readily applied to the equally awesome responsibilities which go with power. One of the things Lyndon Johnson does not miss is "not to have that sergeant with the little black bag a few feet behind me." The sergeant was, of course, the man carrying the codes which could unloose the nation's nuclear force, and the black bag was never farther from the President than was the awful responsibility.

The Johnson transition to private life was better cushioned, however, than that of any previous President. A helicopter and a small jet are on standby for him at the nearest Air Force base. Larger craft would be if he requested them.

He had a special allowance of $375,000 to cover such items as moving and for clerical help to answer the hundreds of letters which continued to pour in for months after he left office.

As a former President he has an annual pension of $40,-000 and an office allowance of $80,000 a year. Additionally there is some $22,000 annually from his Senate retirement, and free medical care and free postage. The secret service men will be around as long as he wants or needs them.

The Johnsons are not troubled about money to meet other expenses, either. Although estimates vary, Lyndon Johnson is certainly several times a millionaire. During the 1964 campaign his accounting firm issued a statement placing the family worth at $3.4 million. More recently the estimates have been between $15 and $20 million. Mr. Johnson's land holdings include some 15,000 acres of ranch land, with six ranch houses, real estate in Austin, banking and other interests and, of course the family television station in Austin, KTBC, which nets a profit of from $100,000 to $200,000 a year.

The Johnson home, the LBJ Ranch, is located a mile up the Pedernales River from the site of Lyndon Johnson's birth. The setting is a land of low-lying hills, with limestone out-cropping, of centuries-old live oaks and stately pecan trees, a country of wild turkey, jack rabbits, raccoons and foxes and deer, as many as thirty-five in one herd. It is also a place of cattle, sheep and goats, but of few ploughed fields. The land is harsh and unkind to planters.

The LBJ Ranch lies in Gillespie County, just over the line of Blanco County. It is some forty-five miles west of Austin, the Capital of Texas, and seventy miles north of San Antonio. To reach the ranch most easily, one goes to Johnson City, named for the President's ancestors, and then drives a dozen miles west on the road to Fredericksburg. En route the motorist passes the village of Hye, where, from an unbelievable red, white and blue, false-fronted, ginger-breaded post office and store building, go some of the mail and supplies to the LBJ Ranch.

A few miles down the road, at a sign "Pedernales Loop," one turns right and strikes an almost parallel road which follows the Pedernales River and leads to Stonewall, where young Lyndon attended grade school a term or two, then across the river to the ranch, entering between two wide stone posts.

Sitting on a rise some seventy-five yards above the river and in a grove of ancient live oaks, is the ranch house. The pillared gallery, or porch, faces the river across a broad lawn of carpet grass. The original part of the house, built by a Johnson relative, is of stone. The newer section, added by the President, is of wood.

In front, to the right as one faces the house, is the contour-edged swimming pool. Farther down and across the cedar fence encompassing the grounds are a barbecue pit and picnic tables. Two other picnic tables sit on the lawn proper. The stock barns are at the left of the house a fair distance away. Behind the ranch house are the landing strip and hangar, both still maintained, and other small buildings.

Life at the LBJ Ranch still moves more or less in the Texas tradition. There are fewer guests these days, and the girls are mostly in their own homes. The days begin much the same in any event, with breakfast of eggs, venison sausage or homecured bacon and home-baked bread, usually served on trays. A door from Mr. Johnson's bedroom opens onto the pool and he may have a swim on first arising. The pool is heated and kept filled the year around.

Concrete stepping blocks leading from the house to the pool bear the names of visitors to the LBJ. One of the oldest carries the name of the President's mother, Mrs. Rebekah Baines Johnson, with the date of December, 1935. There are several with the signatures of foreign guests. The late John Kennedy inscribed his name in 1960. Many of the astronauts are signers, along with other well-known names.

The Johnsons can never expect to be just another of the southeast Texas ranch families living on the Pedernales. The road which passes their ranch home used to be closed by the secret service when they were there in residence. Now, of course, it is open and anyone can stop and picnic in the quiet little parks which grace the miles below the LBJ ranchhouse, or head for the river with a fishing pole. The Johnsons attend church every Sunday and a dozen pastors within a radius of fifty miles possibly attend to their sermons with more care for the former President is virtually non-denominational in his choice of pews to occupy and may pop in on any one of them.

Generally, however, the Johnson neighbors, and in

Texas a neighbor is anyone within a two-hour drive, maintain their own innate dignity and reserve. Any move toward familiarity must come from the former President.

Judge A.W. Moursund is and has been, as these pages noted earlier, probably Lyndon Johnson's closest friend. It is some years since Moursund sat on the Blanco county bench, but in Texas once a judge always a judge. Moursund runs an insurance and law business as well as the bank in Johnson City. At Round Mountain, twelve miles from Johnson City, the Judge also operates one of the largest livestock auction barns in all Texas.

During his years as President, Lyndon Johnson named Judge Moursund chief trustee of the family properties. The Judge's office and home were linked to the ranch and the White House by ten direct telephone lines, including one into the Judge's bathroom. Outside of his immediate family Judge Moursund is probably more frequently at Johnson's side than any other person.

The Johnson daughters, Luci and Lynda Bird, are frequent visitors at the ranch and probably would live there permanently if the former President could have his way. He has always adored his girls and now adores his grandchildren as well.

Luci, now Mrs Patrick Nugent, lives in Austin with her husband and children; a son named Lyndon for his grandfather, but called Lyn and a daughter, Nicole Marie. The Nugents moved to Austin after Patrick completed his military service, including duty in Vietnam, with the Air Force. He is a director of one of the Austin banks and works for the Johnson empire.

Lynda married then Captain and now Marine Major Charles "Chuck" Robb, a professional military man and also a Vietnam veteran. With their two daughters, Lucinda and Catherine, they have established their first home in a Virginia suburb of Washington, D.C.

In addition to his own business affairs and the ranch, two giant-sized projects have occupied the former President since he left the White House: his memoirs, which were sold for $1.5 million, and the truly monumental Johnson Presidential Library on the grounds of the University of Texas. The library was completed in April, 1970.

Construction of the library came under the Presidential Libraries Act, which encourages a President to store his papers in archives financed by private funds and operated by the National Archives, a federal institution.

The Johnson library concept began modestly. The President, as he still then was, thought of it as a small structure in Johnson City; his second choice was his own alma mater, Southwest Texas State College in San Marcos.

Mrs. Johnson, however, foresaw greater possibilities and fewer financial problems in locating it on the huge campus of her own college, the University of Texas in Austin, and probably hadn't too much trouble convincing her husband to agree.

The library, which rapidly grew into a library complex, is a number of things. In addition to the library itself, the complex includes a museum and the Lyndon Baines Johnson School of Public Affairs, intended to prepare graduate students for careers in government. The royalties from Mr. Johnson's memoirs are helping pay for the school.

The library project began in 1965 when then President Johnson selected a 19-acre hillside site on the east side of the university campus. The architectural firms of Skidmore, Owings, and Merrill of New York and Brooks, Barr, Graeber, and White of Austin were selected to design the buildings and they had instructions to bring forth "the best Presidential library in the world."

The result was a library with a tan marble facade, eight stories high and without windows save for the top floor. Its area is 150,000 square feet. Adjoining is the School of Public Affairs, low and long of poured concrete, and containing 275,000 square feet. Together they are both massive and monumental; there have been no complaints about their lack of beauty.

The library will house what is undoubtedly the greatest collection of records and memorabilia (much of it personal) that has ever been collected about any administration or possibly any one man or family. The dozens of vans which had moved out of Washington along the highways to Texas carried:

Thirty-one million sheets of paper, enough to fill 8,000 filing cabinet drawers.

Five hundred thousand photographs of Lyndon Johnson or other members of the family taken by the Official White House Photographer Yoichi Okamoto and two assistants.

Several miles of film, including the home movies taken by Lady Bird of LBJ's first Congressional campaign in 1937.

Transcripts of thousands of phone calls made by Mr. Johnson from the White House.

Timetables of the then Presidential meals, snacks, naps and dips in the White House pool.

Thousands of gifts, from heads of state and from boy scouts, from the rarest of rugs to a mounted moose head.

Headquarters for sifting and sorting and editing the tons of material and the thousands of items was Lyndon Johnson's Austin headquarters on the top floor of the new Federal building there. The Johnson suite includes some 22 offices; four are teak wood paneled and serve Mr. and Mrs. Johnson and their secretaries. Rear office doors in both main offices lead to a bedroom and bath, sitting room with fireplace and dining room and kitchen. An elevator lifts to the helicopter pad on the roof.

Students of history (and tourists) visiting the library will enter through a museum which contains many of the personal items the Johnsons collected during their White House days. Adjacent to the museum are a 1000-seat auditorium and a 200-seat lecture hall.

Above the museum and reached by a marble stair of monumental dimensions is the "great hall," truly heroic in size. The wall opposite the entrance holds five balcony floors of Presidential papers, red-leather bound, under glass and dramatically lighted. Papers of greater public interest are displayed on the ground floor.

Also in the great hall is the most modern of communication devices, the "multi-media center" where the visitor is exposed to photographs, films, cartoons, and the taped recollections of some 500 personages who knew Mr. Johnson. These were collected by at least one full-time interviewer after the library project began. Nearby exhibits demonstrate what Lyndon Johnson considers to be the major achievements of his administration: civil rights, medicare, rural electrification, health and welfare, and space legislation.

In addition to these reminders of his life and his work, the top floor of the library contains offices for Mr. and Mrs.

Johnson. The former President's is an exact reproduction of the oval office he occupied in the White House, and has the same desk he sat at while majority leader of the Senate, with its rows of push buttons to bring every service, from secretary to sandwich.

From the office he can contemplate the future, and some wonder if he will be able to restrain the urge to get back into politics, perhaps run for the Senate again, as another former President did. In any event, he is better equipped in his library than most, to look back upon the past.

Lyndon Johnson's inaugural address in 1965 made the promise of a broad attack on the problems of the poor and the underprivileged—a promise of better housing, education, equal rights and opportunity, plus a drive for improvement in man's environment—clean air and clean water, conservation and beautification.

The "Great Society" never reached the dimensions Lyndon Johnson hoped for it during his time as President, but the historians of years ahead will almost certainly give the Johnson program credit for achieving giant steps in his attempts to "make life better for all Americans."

When Richard Nixon took office he found that his predecessor had left him a legacy of domestic programs which had grown tenfold over the actions he remembered from his days as Vice President.

"There were," said a White House aide to Mr. Johnson, "about 45 domestic social programs when the Eisenhower administration ended. Today there are 435."

Some of them overlap in certain respects, and there is interaction, quite naturally. The more important of them are listed below, by the categories into which they fall most naturally:

EDUCATION

ELEMENTARY SCHOOLS: Elementary and Secondary Act of 1965, strengthened in 1966, providing stepped-up aid to 100 per cent in 1970 for quality education, including textbooks for public and private schools.

HIGHER EDUCATION: Act of 1965 providing liberal loans, scholarships and facility construction money.

TEACHER CORPS: Act of 1965 to train teachers.

AID TO POOR: Educational Opportunity Act of 1968 to help poor go to college.

ADULT EDUCATION: Act of 1968.

JOB OPPORTUNITY

TRAINING: Manpower Development and Training Act of 1964 to qualify persons for new and better jobs.

JOBS CORPS: Economic Opportunity Act of 1964 setting up Job Corps, Neighborhood Youth Corps and new careers programs.

BUSINESS: Job opportunities in the Business Sector, which under the leadership of the National Alliance of Businessmen, seeks 500,000 jobs for hard-core unemployed.

APPALACHIA: Program of 1965 seeking economic development and jobs in an 11 state economically depressed area.

WAGES: Increase in minimum wage by 35 cents to $1.60.

HEALTH

MEDICARE: Set up in 1965, insurance for 20 million citizens at 65 under the Social Security system to cover hospital and doctor costs.

MEDICAID: Act of 1965, providing medical care for the needy, with 7.7 million people in 43 states now getting aid. DOCTOR TRAINING: Health Professions Act of 1963-65 seeking to train 1,700 doctors. NURSES TRAINING: Act of 1964 which has already provided 650,000 loans for schooling. MENTAL HEALTH: Program of 1965-66 providing centers for treatment and training. IMMUNIZATION: Program for preschool children against polio, diphtheria, whooping cough, tetanus and measles. HEALTH CENTERS: Heart, cancer and stroke regional centers. CHILD HEALTH: Improvement and Protection Act of 1968 for prenatal and postnatal care.

CONSERVATION

WATER POLLUTION: Water Quality Act of 1965 and Water Restoration Act of 1966 under which $5.5 billion in grants have been made for water purification and sewage treatment plants. AIR POLLUTION: Clean Air Act and Air Quality Acts of 1965 and 1967 seeking air cleansing through regional grants. WASTES: Solid Waste Disposal Act of 1965. ROADS: Highway Beautification Act of 1965 to cover 75 per cent of the cost of removing roadside eyesores. RECREATION: Urban beautification under the urban renewal act, including the creation of vest pocket parks in congested areas.

PARKS: Expansion of national park system by 2.2 million acres.

ANTIPOVERTY CAMPAIGN

Begun in 1964 with the Economic Opportunity Act and stepped up greatly in later years with the Department of Health, Education and Welfare, the Department of Labor and the Department of Housing and Urban Development.

TRANSPORTATION: Urban mass transportation acts of 1964 and 1966.

MODEL CITIES: Act of 1966 proposing grants to cities, supplemental to those available from other Federal sources, to fight urban problems in the most blighted areas, including those of housing, health, education, jobs, welfare, transportation and public facilities.

RENT SUPPLEMENTS: Started in 1966 to provide better housing for low-income families, funded far below Administration requests.

CRIME CONTROL: Safe Streets and Crime Control Act of 1968, providing block grants to improve state and city law enforcement.

SEGREGATION: Act of 1964 outlawing discrimination in hospitals, restaurants, hotels and employment; authorizing shutoff in Federal aid used in a discriminatory manner.

VOTING: Act of 1965 protecting voting rights at the national, state and local level.

HOUSING: Act of 1968 protecting civil rights workers and initiating fair housing requirements nationally.

COMMUNITY RELATIONS: Transfer of the Community Relations Service from the Commerce to the Justice Department.

CONSUMER PROTECTION

MEAT: Meat Inspection Act of 1967, requiring states to enforce Federal standards or yield to Federal inspection.

POULTRY: Poultry Inspection Act of 1968.

FABRICS: Establishment of Product Safety Commission in 1967 to study dangerous household products and flammable fabrics amendments to 1953 act directing Secretary of Commerce to fix safety standards in clothing.

FARM PRICES: Food Marketing Commission set up to study farm-to-consumer prices.

TRUTH IN LENDING: Act of 1968 requiring dollar-and-cents accounting of actual costs under "easy credit" and other financing plans.

PACKAGING: Fair Packaging and Labeling Act.

ELECTRONICS: Hazardous Radiation Act designed to reduce harmful effects of television and other electronic house devices.

TRAFFIC: Traffic and Highway Safety Act setting standards to be met by manufacturers for automobile safety.

APPENDIX

☆

APPENDIX

APPENDIX

☆

The Johnson Pioneers

In the offices of Lyndon Johnson's personal archivist, in the Executive Offices of the White House, one volume is guarded with particular care.

It is known as "The Mother's Book" and it is never loaned; it is not even shown without the personal permission of the President. "The Mother's Book" is a combination diary and scrapbook kept by Rebekah Baines Johnson, the President's mother.

In it are family records, report cards, newspaper clippings, snapshots and family biographies written by Rebekah Johnson. The volume the President guards and treasures has been much read and handled, and its pages are yellowed and fragile with age. The first page reads:

To Lyndon:
My beloved son, in whom I
find the best of all who have
gone before.
With dearest love and fondest hopes.

          Mother.

May this ancestral history be of interest
as a record of the lives that have gone
into the making of your life, afford you

fuller understanding of the traits of mind
and heart which are your inheritance,
and inspire you to greater heights.

There are report cards from the Johnson City Public Schools.
One, from teacher Carrie Yett, marks Lyndon at age seven with
very good grades indeed—reading a+; spelling a+; writing a;
geography b; deportment wavered from c to b+.

In the fourth grade, age ten, Lyndon received all "a's" except in deportment—a "c." The card shows he was tardy six
times during the semester.

The very first photograph, showing Lyndon as a young baby,
bears a legend in Rebekah Johnson's handwriting:

"When Sam was returning from the home of the neighbor
who took this picture, he raised his hand holding the package
as he saw me waiting on the porch and began to run. I ran to
meet him and we met in the middle of the Benner pasture to
exclaim rapturously over the photograph of our boy. We had
never seen a picture more beautiful—nor did we ever!"

There are several informal snaps of Lyndon at an early age.
In one, at about age five, his mother noted his "golden curls."
Another, taken later, shows him in a ten-gallon hat and a "pensive mood." He is also shown with his cousins at "Uncle Tom's"
and at "Uncle Clarence's" one Christmas. Lyndon and a girl
from the neighborhood were photographed in his first year of
high school. Lyndon is wearing knickers. Both he and the
friend have on black stockings.

The next page pictures him a year later, in 1921, with his
brother and three sisters, and Lyndon is wearing his first pair
of long trousers. The caption notes that he arranged for the
photographer and collected the young members of his family
for the occasion. A 1924 photograph shows Lyndon with the
entire enrollment of the Johnson City High School. He is the
only boy wearing a necktie.

Preserved in the precious scrapbook are pages from the
Southwest State Teachers' College (San Marcos) yearbook,
"The Pedagog." They present Lyndon Johnson as a debater

with a victorious record; as president of the College Press Club; as a senior, with his college major noted as history; and as secretary of the Schoolmaster's Club, an organization devoted to the social and educational benefit of its members.

As part of "The Mother's Book," Rebekah Johnson wrote a biography of her eldest child, the bulk of which is reproduced below. Although it is written in the third person, the words are those of the President's mother.

"It was daybreak, Thursday, August 27, 1908, on the Sam Johnson farm on the Pedernales River near Stonewall, Gillespie County. In the rambling old farmhouse of the young Sam Johnsons, lamps had burned all night. Now the light came in from the east, bringing a deep stillness, a stillness so profound and so pervasive that it seemed as if the earth itself were listening. And then there came a sharp compelling cry—the most awesome, happiest sound known to human ears—the cry of a newborn baby; the first child of Sam Ealy and Rebekah Johnson was 'discovering America.'

"He was a large, well-formed child weighing about ten pounds, the attending physician, Dr. John Blanton of Buda estimated. His Grandmother Baines was first to take him in her arms, calling him a wonderful boy with which Aunt Kate Keele agreed adding that she could see the Bunton favor. Eliza Bunton was his paternal grandmother.

"The proud father—never was there a prouder—assured that all was well with his wife and son, dashed out of the house to saddle Fritz, his splendid grey horse, and gallop up the road to break the glad news, 'it's a boy,' to his parents in the next farmhouse and other kin farther up the road.

"The birth of their son brought great happiness and great changes in the lives of the Sam Johnsons. The father had ardently desired a son and each day his plans and hopes for the boy grew. The mother looked into her son's brown eyes seeing in them not only the quick intelligence and fearless spirit that animated her husband's flashing eyes, but also the deep purposefulness and true nobility that had shone in her father's steady brown eyes. The boy brought new purpose, and greater happiness to her life.

"The baby, the first Baines grandchild but the fifth in the Johnson family, was a great favorite with all the kinfolk. He was bright and bonny, a happy, winsome child, who made friends easily, ate and slept as he should, and woke with a laugh instead of a wail. 'Such a beautiful, such a wonderful baby,' his mother thought early one November morning as she lay watching the baby in his crib beside her bed, and her indignation mounted, 'no name yet.'

" 'Time to get breakfast, Rebekah; the room is warm,' said Sam, lacing his boots by the crackling fire.

"Suddenly Rebekah spoke: 'Sam, I'm not getting up to cook breakfast until this baby is named. He is nearly three months old and the most wonderful baby in the world and still called "Baby." I've submitted all the names I know and you always turn them down. Now you suggest and I'll pass judgment.' Sam was usually the one who issued the ultimatums but Rebekah's, occasional and surprising as they were, achieved results. 'How do you like Clarence?' he asked. 'Not one bit,' came the quick answer, 'try again.' 'Then what about Dayton?' came next. 'Much better; but still not quite right for this boy,' she replied. 'What do you think about Linden for him?' Sam asked. 'That's fine,' was the considered reply, 'if I may spell it as I like. Lin-*den* isn't so euphonious as Lyn*don* Johnson would be.' 'Spell it as you please,' her husband smiled, 'he will still be named for my friend Linden.' 'So now the boy is named Lyndon Baines Johnson. Come cook breakfast; the naming is over.' She kissed the baby's rosy cheek and soon hurried to the kitchen to make the biscuits.

"The first years of Lyndon's life sped swiftly. He was a very active and healthy child and was busy from sunrise to sundown. He loved the farm animals and his dog, 'Bigham Young.' He enjoyed running off to Grandpa Johnson's and eating 'appies' from Grandpa's desk. Grandpa was very proud of this grandson, and predicted a great future for him, writing to his daughter Lucia, out West, 'I have a mighty fine grandson, smart as

you find them. I expect him to be United States Senator before
he is forty.'

"Lyndon liked the farm and rode to school a few miles away
on his pony. He had a group of boy friends all older than he
and usually brought one home to spend the night.

"In 1923 the family returned to their home in Johnson City
so that Lyndon might complete his senior year in school. He
graduated from high school in May 1924. He was the president
of his class of seven. He and Johnnie Brooks Casparis won the
debate in the Blanco County Interscholastic League.

"He had led the normal uneventful, but enjoyable life, of a
popular, fun-loving teen-ager. The Redford and Crider boys
were his closest pals and one, or more, of them was usually
spending the night with him. Now, followed a period of indecision and indifference. His parents were eager for him to
attend college, but his mild interest in books at this time was
discouraging. He had his first job at Robstown. He was restless
and embarked with the Crider and Summy boys on an expedi-
tion to California. This experience of a few months proved a
test of the boy in many ways and helped to clarify his ideas.
He came home and drove a tractor on the highway for some
months.

"This was hard, monotonous work, and his parents felt that
he was wasting time and talents which should have been employed in school. His mother with characteristic persistence
pressed home the fact that work is honorable whether with the
hands or the head, but that education gives opportunity in
every way. One raw cold afternoon, Lyndon came in from a
particularly unpleasant day on the highway and announced,
'I'm sick of working just with my hands and I'm ready to try
working with my brain. Mother, if you and Daddy will get me
in college, I'll go as soon as I can.' His mother walked over to
the phone and called San Marcos Teachers' College to inquire
when the next semester opened. In February 1927, Lyndon
entered college in San Marcos. In August 1930, he received his
degree there having completed during this period three months
of sub-college work, four years of college, and one year of teach-

ing at Cotulla. His grades were excellent, and he was a leader in many extracurricular activities and class administration. He worked in the office of the president of the college and edited the school paper. Inertia and indecision were in the past.

"The next year he taught public speaking in Sam Houston High School in Houston. His debating team went to the State (debating contest) having won the District championship. He loved teaching and was popular with faculty and students.

"In the fall of 1934, he resigned his position in the Houston schools to become Secretary to Congressman R. M. Kleberg. In making this change from teaching to political life, he was aided and abetted by his father whose overwhelming ambition for his son was governmental position. The wisdom of his judgment of Lyndon's ability and aptitude for service in this field has been justified by Lyndon's advancement and success."

(See Family Chart following Appendix)

The parents of Lyndon Baines Johnson were both born in Texas and grew up with the heritage of those frontier Texas days of their youth.

Sam Ealy Johnson, Jr., the fifth child and first son of Sam and Eliza (Bunton) Johnson, was born October 11, 1877 at Buda, Hays County. In his early years, Sam established a country-wide reputation for a memory which achieved almost total recall. When he was still not of school age, he listened to an elder sister memorizing a poem of thirty-two verses for a recital and learned it letter-perfect before she did. He was an active child and loved sports. When he was eleven, the Johnsons moved to Gillespie County, on the Pedernales River, near Stonewall, where young Sam learned to ride, plow and pick cotton along with other boys of the same age.

Money was scarce and Sam's help was needed on the farm, but he was able to attend school most of the term at nearby Johnson City. In her biographical sketch of him, Rebekah Johnson wrote:

"Once his father gave him some cattle saying, 'This is all I can do on your schooling this year.' Each weekend the young high school student turned butcher, slaughtered and cut up a steer and sold steaks and soup bones to tide him over until next 'butchering day.'

"Later on he bought a barber's chair and tools. Soon Sam was a full-fledged barber on Saturdays and afternoons after school."

After graduating from high school, Sam lived a few months with an uncle, Lucius Bunton, in Marfa, West Texas. When he returned from there, his mind was made up to teach school. He spent a few weeks of study with thirteen books covering the required subjects for the examination necessary to a teacher's certificate, and passed the tests.

In the fall of 1896, Sam Johnson taught at the White Oak School in Sandy, Texas. The next year he taught the Rocky School near Hye, Texas. For a while thereafter he rented his father's farm where he lived and achieved a reputation as a genial host. Later, Rebekah Johnson wrote of this:

"Travelers timed their trips to make it to 'Little Sam Johnson's' in order to spend the night and enjoy a good time. 'Little Sam' was six feet but the adjective was used to distinguish him from his father 'Big Sam.' "

In 1904, Sam Johnson was elected to the State Legislature from the 89th District of Texas. He was re-elected for the following term and for four more later on, spending twelve years in the 29th, 30th, 35th, 36th, 37th and 38th Legislatures. Each term was two years.

He was the author of the Alamo purchase bill, a measure appropriating three million dollars to help drought-stricken West Texas ranchers, as well as of a bill providing a home for the widows of Confederate soldiers and of the Johnson Blue Sky law, pertaining to fraudulent representation on the part of vendors. He became famous for a speech on tolerance, delivered on the floor of the Texas House during World War I.

It was an impassioned plea that common sense and justice be applied to the wave of wartime patriotism which had swept the country and reflected his concern for the hundreds of German-American families living in Southwest Texas.

One of his more important legislative votes helped elect a young colleague to be Speaker of the Texas House—Sam Rayburn. Later, of course, Rayburn became Speaker of the United States House of Representatives in Washington, and a friend and counselor of Sam Johnson's son, Lyndon.

In August 1907, Sam married Rebekah Baines, whose father had been his predecessor in the legislature. He had courted her by taking her to reunions of Confederate veterans, where they heard the oratory of such famous Texas spellbinders as Senator Joe Bailey, Senator Charles Culberson and Governor Tom Campbell. Once they listened to William Jennings Bryan, the silver-tongued orator of the Platte, address the Texas legislature.

Rebekah Johnson wrote: "Sam was enchanted to find a girl who really liked politics."

Sam took his bride to the family farm on the Pedernales, where, as recorded in "The Mother's Book," their first son, Lyndon, was born to them on August 27, 1908.

For some years after that Sam engaged in farming, real estate and the cotton brokerage business, along with his political career as a Legislator. Meantime, four other children arrived. They were Rebekah Luruth Johnson, born September 12, 1910; Josefa Hermine Johnson, born May 16, 1912; Sam Houston Johnson, born January 31, 1914; Lucia Huffman Johnson, born June 20, 1916.

Rebekah Luruth Johnson, who followed Lyndon, was born at Stonewall, Gillespie County, September 12, 1910. On May 10, 1941, she married Oscar Price Bobbitt, son of Oscar and Maude Bobbitt of Mineola, Texas. They live in Austin and have one child, Philip Chase Bobbitt, born in Temple, Texas, July 22, 1948.

Josefa Hermine Johnson was born at Stonewall, May 16, 1912. She married Lt. Col. Willard White, at Lake Charles, Louisiana, May 16, 1940, and they were divorced in 1949. She married the Reverend James B. Moss in April of 1955, in Austin, Texas. The couple adopted a child, Rodney Moss, born Biloxi, Mississippi, April 14, 1948. Josefa died in December, 1961.

Sam Houston Johnson, Lyndon Johnson's only brother, was born in Johnson City on January 31, 1914. He was educated as an attorney. He married Albertine Summers, in Mattoon, Illinois, on December 28, 1940, and the two were divorced in 1946. He married Mary Michelson Fish, in Vera Cruz, Mexico, on January 27, 1955. There were two children by the first marriage, Josefa Roxanne, born September 29, 1941, and Sam Summers, born in Austin, October 5, 1942. The Sam Houston Johnsons live in Austin.

Lucia Huffman Johnson was born in Johnson City, June 20, 1916. She was married to Birge Davis Alexander of Sabinal, Texas, on September 18, 1933. Birge Alexander is a construction engineer and the couple lives in Austin with their one child, Rebekah Sterling, born February 13, 1944.

In 1930, Lyndon's father became inspector for the Motor Bus Division of the Texas Railroad Commission. In 1935, he suffered a heart affliction of which he died on October 23, 1936. He was buried in the family graveyard near Stonewall.

Rebekah Baines Johnson, Lyndon's mother, was born June 26, 1881, at McKinney, Texas, the first child of Joseph Wilson Baines and Ruth Ament Huffman. In her autobiography she notes that "my choice of parents was most felicitous; they were a happy, well adjusted, devoted couple who welcomed me into a well ordered, peaceful home to which cross words and angry looks were foreign."

Her father taught Rebekah the multiplication table, to spell and to read at any early age and she attended school in the little town of Blanco, near Johnson City, where her family had moved. Their home was a two-story rock house, where Rebekah lived through her school years, until she left to attend Baylor College.

In the early 1900's, her father suffered a serious financial reverse of which she writes: "We adjusted readily and cheerfully to the financial change. My brother sold his horse and rubber-tired buggy and returned to Texas A & M College where he worked to defray his expenses until he received his degree.

I took charge of the college book store at Baylor College to pay my expenses for my final year there."

Joseph Baines took his family to Fredericksburg in 1904, where he practised law until his death after a lingering illness, on November 18, 1906. Following her graduation from Baylor, Rebekah taught "expression" classes in Fredericksburg. It was at this time that she met Sam Johnson, whom she described as a "dashing and dynamic young legislator."

After the death of her husband, Rebekah Johnson devoted herself to her children and grandchildren until her death on September 12, 1958. She is buried in the family cemetery beside her husband.

Samuel Ealy Johnson, Sr., Lyndon Johnson's paternal grandfather, was born "somewhere in Alabama," on November 12, 1838, the tenth child of Jesse and Lucy Webb Barnett. The family moved to Lockhard, Texas, in 1846.

Orphaned at eighteen, Sam, with his brother Jesse Thomas (Tom), became cattle raisers and drivers, occupations which were traditional to the area and the time. They pastured herds of cattle at Fredericksburg before driving them to market in Kansas. The book, *Trail Drivers of Texas,* notes that they were the largest individual trail drivers operating in 1870 in Blanco, Gillespie, Llano, Burnet, Hays, Comal and Kendall Counties.

Sam enlisted in the Confederate cause in 1861 and served in Company B, DeBray's Regiment, through the Civil War. At the battle of Galveston, his horse was killed under him and he distinguished himself by carrying a wounded comrade on his back from the battlefield.

Returning from the war, Sam married Eliza Bunton, daughter of Lt. Robert Holmes and Jane McIntosh Bunton, on December 11, 1867. The couple set up housekeeping in the little log cabin on the ranch at Johnson City where Sam and his brother, Tom, had formerly "bached."

In addition to the hardships which were normal to the frontier life of a Texas ranch in those days, Indian raids added a fillip of danger all their own. On August 15, 1869, Mr. and

Mrs. Tom Felps, who lived near Cypress Creek, were killed and scalped by Indians. The Felps were Blanco County neighbors and the countryside was aroused and virtually under siege. A few days later, ten men of the section met a band of Indians and the "battle" of Deer Creek ensued. The Indians were routed, but three of the ranchers, Alexander and George Roberts, and Joe Bird were wounded and brought to the Johnson ranch for treatment.

The Johnsons later moved to Caldwell County and then to Buda, in Hays County, where all but the eldest of their nine children were born and attended school. Then in 1889 they returned to the Pedernales River region and settled about twelve miles from Johnson City, where Sam Ealy Johnson, Sr., died of pneumonia on February 15, 1915.

Lyndon Johnson's grandfather was a tall, lithe man, with black wavy hair and blue eyes. In his later years his beard and mane of thick hair became snowy white, giving him a patriarchal appearance. He was noted for his friendliness. Highly gregarious, he attended all neighborly gatherings and usually brought guests home. He always met his friends with a handshake, friendly greeting and hearty laugh.

Eliza Bunton, Lyndon Johnson's paternal grandmother, was born in Russellville, Logan County, Kentucky, on June 24, 1849, the fourth child of Robert Holmes and Priscilla Jane McIntosh Bunton. When Eliza was ten the family moved to Lockhart, Texas, where she met and married Samuel Ealy Johnson. After rearing their family of nine children, Eliza suffered a stroke one February morning in 1912, from which she never fully recovered. She died on January 30, 1917.

Eliza was the niece of John Wheeler Bunton, a signer of the Declaration of Independence and of the Constitution of Texas, a member of the first Texas congress and a hero of the Texas-Mexico battle of San Jacinto. During Indian forays on the ranch, Eliza often saw horses dash into their pens with arrows sticking in their flanks. Sometimes, when left at the ranch alone, she would hide under the cabin floor while the Indians raided the live stock.

She is described as a beautiful, tall woman, with piercing black eyes and coal black hair. She was proud of her family and loved to talk of her cousins, Governor Joseph Desha of Kentucky; the famous Texan, John W. Breckenridge; Mary Desha, co-founder of the Daughters of the American Revolution; and of her brother, Joe Bunton, who fought with the Texas Rangers.

Joseph Wilson Baines, Lyndon Johnson's maternal grandfather, was born on January 24, 1846, in Lebanon, Louisiana, the third son of the Rev. George Washington Baines and Melissa Ann Butler Baines. In 1850, the family moved to Independence, Texas. Joseph was educated at Anderson Academy and Baylor University and fought in the last two years of the Civil War.

In 1867, he began teaching school at Rowlett's Creek, Collin County, where he met Ruth Ament Huffman and married her in 1869. He studied law and started practice in Plano, in 1870, and later in McKinney, where he also published and edited the *Advocate*, an influential Democratic paper. For four years he was Secretary of State under Texas Governor John Ireland.

In 1887, William Baines settled in Blanco and became a member of the 27th Legislature. In 1903, he moved to Fredericksburg, where he died on November 18, 1906.

Baines was a personable man, about five feet, ten inches tall, with brown eyes, brown hair and a complexion tending to ruddiness. He had an excellent sense of organization, saying, "Find the best way to do a thing and always do it that way." He was a devout Baptist and deeply interested in government and politics. He described himself: "I am a Baptist and a Democrat."

Ruth Ament Huffman, the maternal grandmother of Lyndon Johnson, was born December 10, 1854, near Rowlett, Texas, the fifth of eight daughters of Dr. John Smith and Mary Elizabeth (Perrin) Huffman. She attended school and church in Rowlett.

In 1869, just before school opened, Joseph Wilson Baines, Ruth's teacher, asked her mother for permission "to pay his addresses." Shortly before her fifteenth birthday they were married, on September 12, 1869.

In June, 1881, their first child, Rebekah, was born; a second child, Huffman, was born in April, 1884. In 1889, their daughter Josefa, named for her father, arrived. After her husband's death in 1906, Mrs. Baines sold her home and moved with Josefa to San Marcos, Texas, where she boarded college students for several years. She died on February 13, 1936, at the home of her son in San Antonio, Texas.

Lyndon Johnson's great-grandparents were all from the South—Kentucky, Georgia, Louisiana, Tennessee and North Carolina. With one exception, a minister, they were pioneering planters, farmers and colonists. Some were slaveowners.

Jesse Johnson, the father of Sam Ealy Johnson, Sr., was born in Oglethorpe County, Georgia, April 28, 1795. He farmed in Oglethorpe, Henry and Greene Counties and served as sheriff of Henry County. For a brief period in 1838, he and his wife, Lucy Webb Barnett Johnson, lived in Alabama. In 1846, the couple, with eight of their ten children and several slaves, moved to Lockhart, Caldwell County, Texas, where they had bought a home. Jesse died there on May 15, 1856. Samuel Ealy Johnson was his youngest son.

Lucy Webb Barnett, the daughter of Leonard and Nancy Statham Barnett, was born on January 14, 1798, probably in Elbert County, Georgia, although the records are not complete. She is known to have had at least one brother, Pleasant L. Barnett, and probably had other brothers and sisters. She died on March 13, 1857, some ten months after her husband, and was buried beside him in Lockhart, Texas.

Robert Holmes Bunton was a giant of a man, six feet three inches tall and about 260 pounds in weight. He was described as handsome, with a fair skin, coal black hair and piercing black eyes, genial, well-informed and greatly interested in government and politics. He was born September 7, 1818, in Sumner County, Tennessee, the seventh child of Joseph and Phoebe Bunton. He was a substantial planter and owned a number of slaves. He served in the Civil War, finishing as a second lieutenant in Major DeWitt Clinton's battalion. He married Priscilla Jane McIntosh in 1840, in Russellville, Kentucky.

Seven of the eight Bunton children were born in Tennessee, including Eliza, who married Sam Ealy Johnson, Sr. The eighth arrived after the family moved to Lockhart, Texas, in 1858. The family transferred to Stonewall, Gillespie County, in the early 1880's and lived there until Robert's death, on August 22, 1895.

Little is known of the early life of Priscilla Jane McIntosh Johnson. She was born July 8, 1821, in Russellville, Kentucky, the daughter of James William and Julia Ann McIntosh. Of Scottish descent, Priscilla Jane was a diminutive brunette, full of energy and vivacity, quick of movement and sympathy. Her home was a favorite haven for her grandchildren up until the time of her death, on April 28, 1905, when she was nearly eighty-four. She was buried in the Johnson family cemetery near Stonewall.

George Washington Baines, Sr., born near Raleigh, North Carolina, December 29, 1809, was the eldest son of Rev. Thomas Baines and the grandson of Rev. George Bains, an Irish Baptist preacher (who spelled his name without the "e").

The Baines family moved to Georgia in 1817 and the next year to Alabama, where George was reared on a farm without any formal education. After he became of age, he sought and found an education at the University of Alabama, in Tuscaloosa, paying his way by cutting and rafting logs.

At the age of twenty-three, he was converted and baptized, with his license to preach coming in 1834, when he was twenty-five. In 1837, a search for health led him to Arkansas where he became enormously influential as a preacher among the pioneer families who sparsely populated the state. Here George Baines built a log cabin to which he carried his bride, the former Melissa Ann Butler, on the back of his horse, in October of 1840. Although a minister, he was renowned throughout Arkansas for his prowess as a hunter and for his marksmanship in shooting deer and wild turkey. Ten children were born to him and his wife.

In 1844, this pioneer preacher left Arkansas for Mt. Lebanon, Louisiana. After six years he continued on to Texas, settling with his family in Huntsville, where he formed a lifelong friendship with General Sam Houston. He served several pasturates in Texas and became a power among the state's Southern Baptists. During the Civil War he was president of Baylor University, then at Independence. He died of malaria fever, December 28, 1882.

Melissa Ann Butler was described by a friend as "A beautiful young woman with the whitest skin and the blackest hair I ever saw." He also noted that she was modest, reserved and unselfish and that her piety was equaled only by her courage. She was born in North Carolina, June 2, 1824, moved with her family first to Tennessee and thence to Arkansas, where she married George Baines at the age of sixteen. She lived the rugged life of a pioneer woman and sent three sons to the Confederate Army, one of whom died therein. She herself died January 21, 1865, in Fairfield, Texas.

John Smith Huffman, described as a handsome man of medium height, with blue eyes and blond hair, lighthearted, popular and friendly, was born in Bourbon, Kentucky, May 7, 1824. He received a medical degree from the University of Louisville Medical School in 1847, and went to Texas, settling in Collin County. In 1848, he married Mary Elizabeth Perrin and the couple established a home near Rowlett, where they prospered with the fruits of the black land and Dr. Huffman's medical practice. Their farm stock was described as "fine cattle and 100 blooded Kentucky mares." In July, 1863, the young doctor joined Captain Edward Chambers' Company D, 15th Battalion, Texas State Troops. Between the hardships of campaigning and his grief over the lost cause of the Confederacy, Dr. Huffman returned to his home to die on June 22, 1865, leaving his young widow with nine daughters and one son, aged two to sixteen years. He was buried in the Rowlett Cemetery.

Mary Elizabeth Perrin, daughter of William and Dycie Perrin, was born June 27, 1826, in Russellville, Kentucky, the fourth in a family of ten children. All of them went to Texas with their parents in 1845 or '46, locating in Collin County. Mary Elizabeth is described as comely and industrious, small, with black hair and eyes. Widowed in 1865, at the age of thirty-nine, and left with nine daughters and a son to support, she managed to carry on the work of the farm, and educate and marry off her children. She lived to the age of ninety, dying in Merkel, Texas, on July 12, 1916.

The roots of Lyndon Johnson go deep into the South. Of the sixteen great-great-grandparents listed here on the chart, the majority were from North Carolina and the others came from Kentucky. As in most genealogical charts, possibilities of errors here must be admitted.

John Johnson was of English descent but his residence prior to 1795 is unknown, as is the name of his first wife and mother of his six children. He was living in Oglethorpe County, Georgia, in 1795. On May 24, 1823, he married Joicy Bowdrie Fears, the widow of William Fears. He participated in the land lottery of 1827 and was awarded 202½ acres in Lee County. He served in the Revolutionary War. It is interesting to note that in his will, each of his two daughters was bequeathed "one Negro girl."

Joseph Robert Bunton was born about 1782, in Rowan County, North Carolina, the son of John and Mary Elizabeth (McClure) Buntin. (The spelling changes.) Before 1800, he moved with his father to Sumner County, Tennessee, where he engaged in farming. He met and married Phoebe Ann Desha in 1804. The couple reared a family of eight in Sumner County; there, in the early 1840's, Joseph Bunton died and was buried.

Phoebe Ann Desha was born in 1784, near the Kentucky

border. The daughter of Robert and Elinor (Wheeler) Desha, she was among the younger of twelve children. Her brother Joseph, born in 1768, was Congressman from Kentucky from 1806 to 1819 and Governor of Kentucky from 1824 to 1828. Robert, born in 1777, was Congressman from Tennessee from 1827 to 1831. Two other brothers were killed by Indians while in their youth. In the early days of the Texas Republic, Mrs. Phoebe Bunton, now a widow, followed her sons, who had settled in Lockhart and Hays County. Taking along a number of slaves, she made her home in Bastrop. The 1860 census records her as a widow of seventy-six, residing in the home of her son, James Monroe Bunton. A few years later, she died at the home of her son, John Wheeler Bunton, at Mountain City, Hays County, Texas.

Thomas Baines, father of George Washington Baines, was born in Edenton, North Carolina, July 4, 1787. He was the youngest son of George and Mary Baines. On February 13, 1808, he married a young Scottish girl, Mary McCoy. He and an elder brother, James, were ordained as Baptist ministers in Georgia on August 22, 1817. About a year later, the Thomas Baineses moved to Alabama where he was pastor of many rural churches. In 1836, he transferred his family to Mississippi. He died that same year, after leading the busy life of a pioneering preacher for less than fifty years. He had four children. The eldest son also became a Baptist minister. It was Thomas who changed the family name from Bains to Baines.

Mary McCoy Baines, mother of George Washington Baines, was born in Perquiman County, North Carolina, in 1783, the youngest of seven children of William and Julia McCoy. Her grandfather was James McCoy, who pioneered from Scotland. As stated, she married Thomas Baines in 1808 and followed him to Georgia, Alabama and Mississippi. After the death of her husband, she lived with her youngest son, Joseph B. Baines, in Harrison County, Arkansas, and later with her eldest, Rev. George W. Baines, in Fairfield, Texas, where she died in 1864.

Nealy Butler, father of Melissa Ann Butler, was born in

North Carolina, on January 15, 1796. While a young man, he married Amy Ogier, taking her to Tennessee. About 1836, he moved his family to Carroll County, Arkansas, where he farmed until shortly after the Civil War. The Butlers had ten children. On the secession of Arkansas from the Union—being in favor of the Union of the States—Nealy Butler migrated north to Stone County, Missouri, in order to protect his family. He remained here until his death in 1880.

Amy Ogier, wife of Nealy Butler, was born in North Carolina, on February 28, 1799. She came from a long and illustrious line, a descendant of the French Huguenot family of Louis and Catherine (Creuze) Ogier, silk merchants who came to Carolina with their nine children on the ship, *Union,* in February 1774.

John Smith Huffman, great-grandfather of Rebekah Baines, was born in Bourbon County, Kentucky, on November 2, 1794. He was first married in 1818, to Suzanne Ament, by whom he had seven children; secondly to Lucinda Armstrong, in 1831, by whom he had five children; and thirdly to Helen Hall, a new England school teacher, in 1844, a union which produced no offspring. He farmed successfully in Kentucky until 1851, then moved to Texas and settled in Collin County where he accumulated a large land estate. He was the first to breed short horn cattle successfully in Texas and the first to introduce the Sir Archer breed of horses to the state. Up until the time of his death, at the age of eighty-five, on October 7, 1880, his erect form, clear blue eyes and thick white hair made a striking and familiar figure as he rode through his Texas fields astride his horse. He is buried in the Rowlett cemetery.

Suzanne Ament, first wife of John Smith Huffman, was born in 1801, in Bourbon County, Kentucky, near the Fayette County line. She died in May, 1831, when her twin daughters, Mary and Martha, were only one year old. Her father was of French extraction and a soldier in the Revolutionary War. She was a gentle, vivacious and sprightly brunette.

Going five generations back to the great-great-great-grand-parents of Lyndon Baines Johnson, the records are quite natu-rally incomplete and uncertain as to their accuracy. The following people are among those ancestors and the details may or may not be entirely correct.

Nathan Barnett, born in 1729, in Greene County, Georgia, served as a Revolutionary soldier and was awarded a "bounty grant" of land. He had married Lucy Webb in 1757 and the couple had at least five children, four of whom served also in the Revolution, including Nathan, Jr. Nathan, Sr. died in 1798.

George Bains, born January 26, 1741, may have been the emigrant ancestor of the Baines family, having come from Scotland to Chowan County, North Carolina, in his youth. He was a surveyor, a planter and a well-educated man for the times. He served in the Revolution, was called "Blackbeard" to distinguish him from others of the Bains (and Baines) fam-ilies in the neighborhood. He married Mary Creecy on May 28, 1769, and reared eleven children. He died on May 19, 1802, and his will, dated May 7, 1802, is interesting for some of its bequests. They include the sum of twelve pounds to be paid annually to his widow and twenty-five shillings left to each of several children, with plots of land to others. His widow also was to have a life estate in his plantation, for which he left detailed instructions regarding certain repairs to the chimneys of the house.

Robert Desha, born about 1740, in Monroe County, Penn-sylvania, was a descendent of the Huguenots of France, from where his father fled to escape persecution. About 1760, Rob-ert Desha married Eleanor Wheeler. In 1781, they emigrated to Kentucky and the following year to Tennessee where they became the parents of twelve children and where Robert Desha attained a position of influence and property. One son, Robert, was a Congressman from Tennessee; another, Joseph, became Congressman and Governor of Kentucky. Desha was a private in the Revolution and received a grant of 640 acres of land in Sumner County, Tennessee, near Bledsoe's Lick. He died there in the fall of 1816.

His will, dated the May before his death, made several sizable cash bequests and others of land; it parcels out numerous slaves, their present children and future get, and leaves each of his own children one hundred dollars in cash to purchase suitable mourning attire.

John Buntin II, the son of John Buntine I (note change of spelling), with his father and two brothers, fought in the Revolution. His birth date is unknown. He first married Mary McClure Buntin, whose death is unrecorded. He settled on 640 acres of land on Bledsoe Creek, Sumner County, Tennessee, on January 4, 1800, with three children. John Buntin died in 1803.

His will left his second wife, Elizabeth, a life estate on the farm as long as she remained his widow, along with "my Negro whench Luce, a horse worth eighty dollars, her saddle and bridle, two beds and furniture, my table furniture, big trunk, also my pots, bake oven, pot rack and tongs, pails and wash tubs; also I give her the use of the cupboard during life, then to belong to my son Joseph." The remainder of the estate went to his son Joseph, except for bequests of two dollars each to his daughter Sarah and his son, William, and of one red heifer to his grandson, John Kerr.

John Buntine I, an emigrant from Scotland, came to Rowan County, North Carolina, in 1758, where he purchased a section (640 acres) of land and reared three sons, John II, Robert and James. He later dropped the "e" from his name and eventually it became Bunton. John Bunton I was the first of the American line which dates back to Finlay Bunting, who in 1398 received from Robert the Third of Scotland a grant of land in Dumbartonshire which he named Airdrock. One of John Buntine I's descendants, John W. Bunton, was a signer of the Declaration of Independence of Texas in 1836.

He was Lyndon Johnson's great-uncle.

FAMILY CHART OF

Lyndon Baines Johnson

This chart has been made as complete and accurate
as possible. Naturally, some of the far back
records are missing or uncertain.

LYNDON BAINES JOHNSON

Sam Ealy Johnson
FATHER
B Oct. 11, 1877, Buda, Tex.
D Oct. 22, 1937, Austin, Tex.
M Aug. 20, 1907
W Fredericksburg, Gillespie Co.,
Tex.

Samuel Ealy Johnson
GRANDFATHER
B Nov. 12, 1838, Alabama
D Feb. 25, 1915, Stonewall, Tex.
M Dec. 11, 1867
W Lockhart, Tex.

Jesse Johnson
GREAT GRANDFATHER
B Apr. 28, 1795, Georgia
D May 15, 1856, Lockhart, Te
M Nov. 14, 1817
W Greene Co., Ga.

Lucy Webb Barnett
GREAT GRANDMOTHER
B Jan. 14, 1798, Georgia
D Mar. 3, 1857, Lockhart, Te

Eliza Bunton
GRANDMOTHER
B June 24, 1849, Russellville, Ky.
D Jan. 30, 1917, Stonewall, Tex.

Robert Holmes Bunton
GREAT GRANDFATHER
B Sept. 17, 1818, Tenn.
D Aug. 22, 1895, Stonewall, T

Jane McIntosh
GREAT GRANDMOTHER
B July 8, 1821
D Apr. 28, 1905, Stonewall, T

Rebekah Baines
MOTHER
B June 26, 1881, McKinney, Tex.
D Sept. 12, 1958

Joseph Wilson Baines
GRANDFATHER
B Jan. 24, 1846, Mt. Lebanon, La.
D Nov. 18, 1906, Fredericksburg,
Tex.
M Sept. 12, 1869
W Rowlett, Collin Co., Tex.

George Washington Baines
GREAT GRANDFATHER
B Dec. 29, 1809, N.C.
D Dec. 28, 1882, Belton, Tex.
M Oct. 20, 1840
W Carroll Co., Ark.

Melissa Ann Butler
GREAT GRANDMOTHER
B June 2, 1824, N.C.
D Jan. 21, 1865, Fairfield, Tex

Ruth Ament Huffman
GRANDMOTHER
B Dec. 10, 1854, Collin Co., Tex.
D Feb. 13, 1936, San Antonio,Tex.

John Smith Huffman
GREAT GRANDFATHER
B May 7, 1824, Kentucky
D June 22, 1865, Collin Co. Te
M 1848, Collin Co., Tex.
W Collin Co., Tex.

Mary Elizabeth Perrin
GREAT GRANDMOTHER
B June 27, 1826, Kentucky
D July 12, 1916, Merkel, Tex.

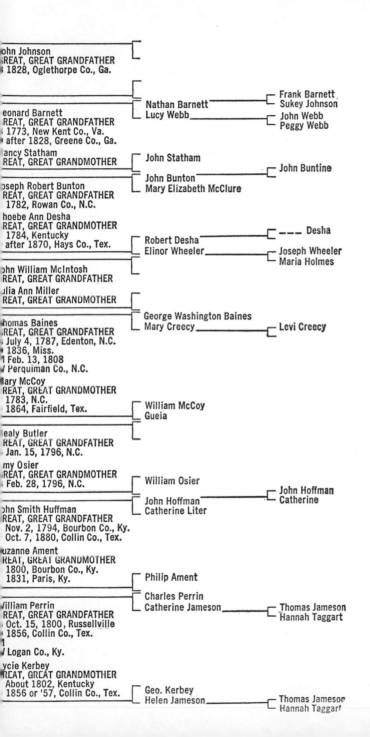

John Johnson
GREAT, GREAT GRANDFATHER
1828, Oglethorpe Co., Ga.

Nathan Barnett ——— Frank Barnett
Lucy Webb ——— Sukey Johnson
—— John Webb
Peggy Webb

Leonard Barnett
GREAT, GREAT GRANDFATHER
1773, New Kent Co., Va.
after 1828, Greene Co., Ga.

Nancy Statham
GREAT, GREAT GRANDMOTHER

John Statham

John Bunton ——— John Buntine
Mary Elizabeth McClure

Joseph Robert Bunton
GREAT, GREAT GRANDFATHER
1782, Rowan Co., N.C.

Phoebe Ann Desha
GREAT, GREAT GRANDMOTHER
1784, Kentucky
after 1870, Hays Co., Tex.

Robert Desha ——— ___ Desha
Elinor Wheeler ——— Joseph Wheeler
Maria Holmes

John William McIntosh
GREAT, GREAT GRANDFATHER

Julia Ann Miller
GREAT, GREAT GRANDMOTHER

George Washington Baines
Mary Creecy ——— Levi Creecy

Thomas Baines
GREAT, GREAT GRANDFATHER
July 4, 1787, Edenton, N.C.
1836, Miss.
Feb. 13, 1808
Perquiman Co., N.C.

Mary McCoy
GREAT, GREAT GRANDMOTHER
1783, N.C.
1864, Fairfield, Tex.

William McCoy
Gueia

Sealy Butler
GREAT, GREAT GRANDFATHER
Jan. 15, 1796, N.C.

Amy Osier
GREAT, GREAT GRANDMOTHER
Feb. 28, 1796, N.C.

William Osier

John Hoffman ——— John Hoffman
Catherine Liter ——— Catherine

John Smith Huffman
GREAT, GREAT GRANDFATHER
Nov. 2, 1794, Bourbon Co., Ky.
Oct. 7, 1880, Collin Co., Tex.

Suzanne Ament
GREAT, GREAT GRANDMOTHER
1800, Bourbon Co., Ky.
1831, Paris, Ky.

Philip Ament

Charles Perrin
Catherine Jameson ——— Thomas Jameson
Hannah Taggart

William Perrin
GREAT, GREAT GRANDFATHER
Oct. 15, 1800, Russellville
1856, Collin Co., Tex.

Logan Co., Ky.

Lycie Kerbey
GREAT, GREAT GRANDMOTHER
About 1802, Kentucky
1856 or '57, Collin Co., Tex.

Geo. Kerbey
Helen Jameson ——— Thomas Jameson
Hannah Taggart

Index

241

92
JOH
NEWLON, CLARKE
L.B.J., the man from
Johnson City. Rev.

DATE DUE			
FEB 23	APR 3	4	
MAR 19	APR 21	4	
APR 2	APR 29		
MAY 2	MAY 28		
OCT 14	NOV 22		
MAR 3	DEC 22		
FEB 27	JAN 20		
MAR 1	12/14/95		
NOV 27			
APR 17			
MAY 22			ALESCO